A New World With God!

Fumiko Nomura

たま出版

The Kanzeon Bosatsu
(Kanzeon Bodhisattva) appears

Refer to "Chapter 2 Seoritsuhime-sama"

Refer to "The anaconda which became reunited with its family"

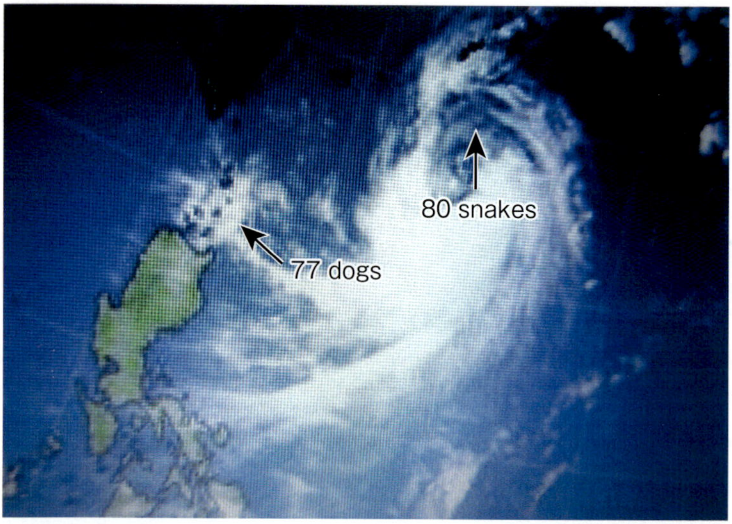

Refer to “Various events that occurred along with Typhoon 22”

Four dragon gods who helped in typhoons 5/18/21/22

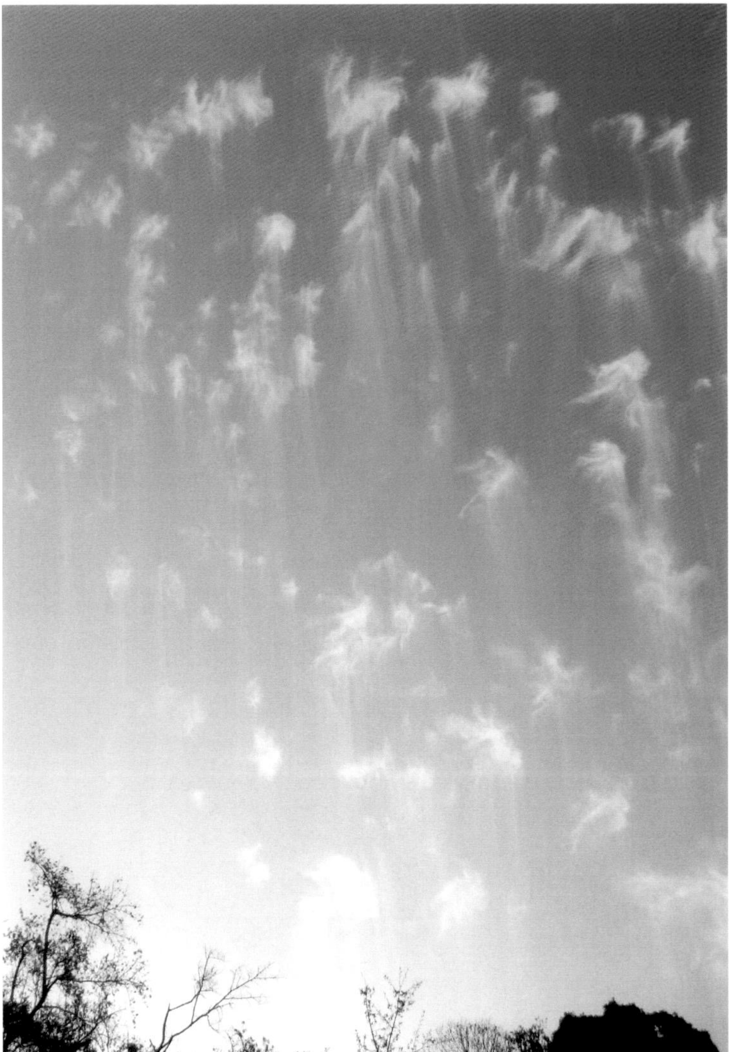

The ascension of 32 pigs (female)

The ascension of 28 bulls

The ascension of 33 male spirits

A pine tree dying because of parasites

Hand Power!

A miraculous recovery

Wilting from possession of thought-energy of cataract from diabetes (egg plant seedlings)

Recovered from the removal of the thought-energy (egg plant seedlings)

Introduction

Seventeen years ago, I had my first contact with waves that cannot be seen by the naked eye, and was fascinated by the wave measuring instrument that could measure these waves. Furthermore, I invented the idea of an original purging method called "Future Waves."

What was setting me in motion was the regret I felt from the loss of my eldest son at the age of one year and one month. Eventually, as I was studying the waves, I was able to reveal the reason of my son's death, and experienced a magical occurrence where the soul of my eldest son entered in to the body of my second son. The joy I felt came short, for my second son started having symptoms of the same illness as before. With earnestness to this time save his life, I poured in all of the experience I had gained since, and actually did save his life using the power of purification of the unseen waves.

In this process, with the help of God, what evolved was the "Card of Hikari." The purging power increased overwhelmingly, and the method became simplified. From 2016, it was discovered that chronic illnesses were formed as gaps at the forehead of that person. With people who have many, there can be a data accumulation of 50 gaps. Also, if images of blood samples are analyzed at 3600 times magnification, the cause of illness, factual realities of DNA, personality disorders, etc. can be meticulously clarified. This will be explained further in the first chapter. As of now, purifying the forehead alone can allow purification of the whole body.

These efforts have bared fruit, and now, as a continuation of the publications of "The Truth of Life Discovered by Waves" (Tama Publishing) on August 11th, 2005, and "The True Nature of Illness Taught by Future Waves" (Tama Publishing) on April 1st, 2010, it has become possible to reveal many truths to the world through this new book. In chronological order, real conversations with gods will be introduced.

This time there is also an important notice that must be given. When the due date of the manuscript of this book became near, a new fact became clear. Since now I have discovered the cause of illnesses to be from spirits, bacteria, viruses, and cosmic spirits, but there were areas where that were unclear. I have been naming these other areas as "other causal factors," but when I studied the cause of an illness of a particular female, it all became clear. What had once been unclear as a cause of illness was the existence of cells that had been genetically engineered.

I became staggered by this, and studied other members of our School of Unseen Waves, and felt myself turn pale as I realized that the members who were right there also had a great amount of genetically engineered cells inside them. Because these cells have no name, I began referring to them as "cells" and studied them further. It turned out that these cells were included in a wide range of places, for example pharmaceutical products, health products, tea, and food. They can also be found in food that are not labeled as genetically engineered.

The features associated with a Cell were various, including lethargy, neurological abnormality, pain, symptoms found in the entire brain, anemia, obesity, vomiting, and diarrhea. Around that time, the gun violence incident in Las Vegas resulting in 59 people dead and 500 people wounded occurred, which was reported as a historical catastrophe. The suspect apparently committed suicide, but I found in his forehead 15 cells carrying neurological abnormality, along with an angry male cosmic spirit.

Currently, children and young people struggle with illnesses with no medical explanation, allergies, hay fever, decrease in visual ability, and lethargy, which are things that did not occur in the past. Being surrounded by such kinds of food has lead to this erosion. When the number becomes high, people acquire the same personality and disease as what they are being possessed by. If humanity keeps going in this direction, we may experience such catastrophes or incurable diseases every day. The reality is that because we do not know the mechanism of these things, we are unable to even understand how to solve these problems.

If you were to practice purification using unseen waves,

horrible cells can also be purged. I invented the idea of Future Waves, but this technique is not something that I alone can only do. Anybody in the world can do it. Actually the members of my School of Unseen Waves are already doing it, utilizing the method for purifying themselves, their family, people in their environment, and their environment itself.

There is an immeasurable number of cells, spirits, bacteria, viruses, and cosmic spirits that exist as cause of illnesses. I wish with earnestness that everybody learns the truth through this book, and to practice the purification method of unseen waves for the future of humankind.

Table of Contents

Introduction ··· 1

Chapter 1 Cause of Illness Can Be Found Deep Within the Third Eye

What are Waves? ··· 10

Almost all of a person's information can be found at the forehead·········· 12

Regarding people who have gods in their forehead ··························· 15

The cause of chronic illnesses found in blood sample images magnified by 3600 times ··· 18

Many illnesses that are given the word "intractable disease" ················· 23

Incredible knowledge that can be attained ······································ 29

The truth which was discovered through the mortuary tablet··············· 35

Conversations with bacteria and viruses are possible························· 39

Japan, the nation of people drugged by pharmaceutical products ·········· 43

Chapter 2 Ro-Ne-Ra-Wa-Yu-Wa (Conversations with Gods)

Seoritsuhime-sama ··· 48

Your behavior before life becomes reflected in your afterlife················ 58

The purification of spirit-groups·· 61

The purification of Plutonium ··· 68

More than 37000 gods of the world!··· 71

"Light shall come from the East": this means the light of God·············· 75

Christ, Mohammed, and the Buddha··· 79

Iron Balls Falling ··· 81

Regarding the sixteen princes·· 84

The legend of Yamato no Orochi and Susano-nomikoto-sama ············· 88

Amaterasuoomikami-sama·· 92

Thirty-seven gods (a genealogy of gods, 17 gods and 20 living gods) ······ 94

The legend of the Inaba Rabbit and Okuninushiookami-sama ············· 97

To be completely guide by God·· 98

Cosmic spirits and their increase·· 100

Chapter 3 A Dream Story and the Unknown World

How a god entered in to my dream which then came true ·················· 106
The bond between cosmic spirits and anacondas······························ 107
The anaconda which became reunited with its family························ 119
How ancestors also experience hell ·· 124
A true "kamikakushi," or spiritual disappearance ···························· 128
How she experienced pain every day·· 130
Asking help from a dragon god regarding the huge Typhoon 5 ············· 133
Revelations from God ··· 140
Mercury, Planet Nanronu, Planet Warayamori……conversations with cosmic spirits ·· 143
Conversations with angels ··· 150
Conversations with animal spirits ··· 151
The New Year of 2017 for my ancestors·· 159
A story about a person becoming a bacterium··································· 162

Chapter 4 The Afterlife

My child who was born after 42 years!·· 168
Studies of the soul upon the death of my beloved cat Musashi·············· 175
People who have become possessed by foxes ··································· 178
Daily life of ancestors and conversations with them ·························· 180
Someone who lived in the 2nd floor of our house····························· 185
The issues of a person who was a detective in a previous life ··············· 187
Thanks to my 100 year old beloved cat··· 191
Conversation with a satanic spirit who dwelled inside blood················ 198

Chapter 5 Experiences Having to do with Anybody Being Able to Purge

ALS myasthenia disease ·· 202
A kidney stone 25 km away disappeared through teleportation············ 204
The experience of my 82 year old mother with cholangitis·················· 208
Hands that turned bright yellow and the inability to stop eating snacks ·· 213
The cause of a week-long tooth ache within the ear ························· 217
Life after resurrection from being a drugged corpse·························· 220

The experience of a complete purification even from a long distance······ 225
An intractable disease found only in 3 patients in the world, including 1 in Japan, easily cured······ 227
The discoveries, practices, and problem-solving ability of Nomura Sensei who leads the pathway to the future······ 230
My experience······ 235

Chapter 6 The Way of Salvation is to Surrender to the Guidance of God
The cause of the Tottori earthquakes······ 242
The cause of the Kumamoto earthquake······ 243
The first plea towards dragon gods with Typhoon 18······ 246
The animals that were in Hurricane Irma······ 250
Various events that occurred along with Typhoon 22 (Oct. 27th, 2017)··· 252
The nuclear threat from North Korea, defeated by the power of God!······ 253
[New Information: discovery of nuclear cells that could destroy humanity!]······ 270
Message from Amaterasuoomikami-sama: "Re-e-ta-ki-ru-na-ke-i-a-a-ya-fu-ha-sa"······ 277

Chapter 7 Seventeen-years history of Future Waves

"I have received a final message from the Space Creator deity" Final Message from the Space Creator deity (King of the Gods, Amaterasuoomikami, Seikannon, YHVH, Jehova and Allah)······ 294

In Closing······ 309

補足······ 315

Chapter 1

Cause of Illness Can Be Found Deep Within the Third Eye

What are Waves?

To understand the content of this book, first you must know what waves are. As I have written in my other books, they are the origin of all things including human beings, minerals, and plants.

It is known in modern science that the human body can be broken down in to cells, molecules, atoms, down to subatomic particles (the neutrino and top fork). Beyond subatomic particles exist cosmic energy, where there are waves, qi, and physiognomy. All things such as animals, plants, minerals, photographs, buildings, and land come from qi, and this can be captured through a wave measurement device.

I use the LFA (Life Field Analyzer) wave measurement device. Most wave measurement devices display values of positive 20 (high energy) and negative 20 (low energy), negative values meaning bad and positive values meaning good.

For example, if you were to be possessed by a thought-energy that is negative 3, there is some pain but not anything the you could not withstand, so with endurance you could still work. However, if the negative value goes beyond that level, there is more that is possessing, and the pain could exacerbate to the point of being unbearable. When these things are removed, the body is restored.

The LFA wave measurement device I use displays 4-digit

numbers or in codes written in combination with alphabets and numbers in a detailed manner, towards all fields such as the nervous system, digestive system, respiratory system, infections, bacteria, emotions, chakras, colors, vitamins, food, and insects. You just choose the word that describes what you want to measure, an input the code number of that word in to the wave measurement device, and see if it comes out as positive or negative.

The device does not necessarily have detailed information within it for each code number, but somehow, magically, it matches everything in reality. With photos of cancer, bacteria, and viruses, the measurement also produces the result "cancer", "bacteria", or "virus." In the case of criminals, the measurement results in "rage" and "falseness."

In this way, whether spirits, bacteria, or viruses are possessing a person, animal, plant, or food can be detected, along with the quantity, is possession is the case. In this book, there will be given many numerical values. These values have been measured by me with a sensor. There are differences between people, but if everything is measured, the basic data will match. Please know that all of the data given in this book are from the results of measurements made by me personally.

Almost all of a person's information can be found at the forehead

The way of practicing Future Waves is to remove and purify the spirits, bacteria, and/or viruses of a person, animal, or object upon the measurement of waves.

What is used during the purification is the Card of Hikari (the light of God) which had achieved its form of completion upon trial and error while consulting with gods. The method of its usage is quite simple. Just put the card on a photo (it is also fine to use the image being shown on the camera itself) from 5 to 10 minutes. It has been proven that when using the wave measurement device, bacteria, viruses, spirits, and even radiation will disappear.

As I continued my research, it became known that what was before undetectable could then be detected. It was in the year 2016. Also, I should tell you that once the Card of Hikari is removed from the wave measurement device, the device returns to being a general wave measurement device, and the measurement becomes superficial.

What I began to see was the data regarding the entire body of that person in their forehead. From way in the past, the Buddha has had a mark on his forehead. It is known in Buddhism as the Yintang, in yoga as the focal point of energy, also as one of the major chakras. Upon searching for what really is within the forehead, and to what degree, I found out that there were 14 different layers piled up in my forehead. In those layers were inputted bacteria, viruses, ageing, toxins, sadness, obsession, and matched the symptoms that I had in the back of my left knee, left buttock, eyes, and the bags under my eyes,

The symptoms were all a part of what was like a chronic disease that I had had since youth, like cataract, hippocampus, arteriosclerosis, metabolic malfunction, urinary incontinence, hernia, negative theta waves, congestion, dermatological malfunction.

But of course, I had been purified from before, so those were just what were left over and the quantity was low, and they had not been affecting me. However, due to the results I consistently purify them all.

Later on, I measured the foreheads of celebrities on television. On person had 11 layers in their forehead. In separate layers there were spirits, viruses, and sometimes the same bacteria. The person was possessed by a spirit whose personality consisted of negativity in terms of self-centeredness, morality, cooperation, thankfulness, and intentions. Also, the person was possessed by a fox that is too pride and hysterical, and these personalities came out through the person possessed. It seemed, though, that if these things were purified, this person could be like a gentleman. His illness was caused by bacteria that made him fatigued, but his condition was not critical.

I also measured the same person after ten days. This time, there were 21 layers, with two new animals. Other than that, there were the same results as before. Later on, after studying the foreheads of various people, I began to discover that some people had 20 layers or even 50 layers.

This means a lot of work. If one layer were to take five minutes to purify, 12 layers would take an hour. With people who have many layers, after purifying one layer, another layer would occur from their bloodstream, and therefore purification must be one all day.

Because of this, I decided to perform a certain experiment. At night, I placed a photograph of myself in between two Cards of Light and went to sleep. Everything that was inputted was purified and became clean by morning. For people who have much information to be inputted, they could take another picture in the morning, place it in between Cards of Light, an go to work or do their house chores. From this I came to the conclusion that people must do self-purification.

On February 2017, a certain religion was televised amply. There, the same spirit that caused delusions were in the first, second, or fifth layers of head staff members and passionate believers. I realized that this is the reason why people can share beliefs and work together as a religious organization.

Regarding people who have gods in their forehead

The waves of spirits stop at positive 20, but while making measurements with foreheads of people, we were able to make the measurement of positive 4 billion.

This measurement cannot be made with a usual wave measurement device. A Card of Hikari with high waves must be placed on top of the device. There are various cases where gods are in possession of these people, for example a male god, a female goddess, or a god that is both a god and a goddess (the great Kanzeon Bosatsu(Kanzeon Boddhisattva)), or two goddesses. There can be cases where even more gods are in possession. Also, an androgynous being (an angel) whom has a very high wave measurement could also be with a person.

I have made measurements with many people in the past, such as people who are in my life directly, celebrities, politicians, entertainers, and athletes. Through the experiences of making these measurements, I found those who are selfless and thankful are in possession of gods, and this makes sense.

As I looked across the world, Nobel Peace Prize winners such as Martin Luther King, Eisaku Sato, Mother Teresa, Nelson Mandela (former president of South Africa), Kim Dae-jung, President Obama, Liu Shaopo, Malala Yousafzai, Gorbachev (former Soviet Union president), along with John Paul II, Chiune Sugihara, Princess Diana, Boris Yeltsin (first

Russian president), Weizsäcker(former German president), were possessed by gods.

I will not give their names, but many of the athletes who competed well in the Olympics of Rio de Janeiro in Brazil were also possessed by gods. Perhaps they were given the role of being a symbol of effort and spirit for the world. Also, recently there are physicians from the medical world who are sounding an alarm towards modern medicine. There are books published that take risk of losing the dogmatic beliefs that have been had towards Western medicine, but these authors are possessed by gods in most cases. To fight for truth while sacrificing oneself is, I believe, a quality that shows that gods are at work.

The emperor of Japan and his spouse, along with the crown prince and spouse, are each possessed by the Kanzeon Bosatsu. I would also like to note that it is said that the world was created with Japan as a prototypical model, and that sixteen princes were sent from Japan to various locations in the world, and foundations of nations were built by them. As proof of this, recently a coat of arms with the chrysanthemum, a symbol of Japan, has been found with buried goods excavated from the Egyptian pyramid. I have confirmed this truth through conversations with gods (refer to Chapter 2 Ro-Ne-Ra-Wa-Yu-Wa (Conversations with Gods)/Seoritsuhime-sama).

In other words, the people of this world are all brothers and sisters with blood relations. If this is the case, we must stop robbing land and other resources from each other. There are regions in this world where "naughty children" have grown. Japan, as the parent nation, should teach about propriety, but people are not willing to listen.

With this in mind, as I find out that evil spirits wit negative thought-energy are possessing the heads of various nations, I purify as much as I can with the help of God. By just allowing the light to touch the face for five minutes, the negative thought-energy can be instantly transformed into positive thought-energy. Then, that particular individual begins to be conscientious.

Also, as a cause of hurricanes, typhoons, and earthquakes, the tragic anger and stress of animals, their pain, fatigue, and other forms of suffering are often evident. I also purify them and release them to the heavens. However, what I do not wish is to be complacent with the thought that "somebody is taking care of things.

God wants us to realize why military conflicts and earthquakes occur, what the root cause is. I feel that it is God's message for us to realize the reasons why disease, crime, and disasters occur, and to purify this root cause as we learn from our past mistakes, and to prevent these causes from occurring in the future. Especially, I feel that God would like us to teach children about it.

The writing of this book has been supervised by God, and

mistakes have been corrected while lacking information have been added. Please know that this book also contains the will of God.

The cause of chronic illnesses found in blood sample images magnified by 3600 times

In the past, I had a particular doubt.

One time, I had been purifying myself because I found out that I was infested with spirits, bacteria, and viruses. But however much I would purify myself, they would come out again. When I started doubting whether I was succeeding in purifying myself, a certain thought occurred to me. Perhaps these things are in my bloodstream?

I remembered taking photos of blood samples together with my family in the past, and searched for them at once and measured them. I realized that even one drop of blood could be infested. The reason why I was having trouble purifying was because they kept multiplying in my blood.

An example that made this clear was through the observation of my blood sample image with a microscope that zoomed in to the level of 3600 times. A company in Aichi prefecture provides the service of taking blood sample images zoomed in at the level of 3600 times. With this image, the cause of illness, facts about your DNA, and any problems with personality can be revealed in detail. I recommend it to everybody. Also, I have written a thesis regarding the measurement results of the blood of seven representatives from my School of Waves, and plan to announce it at another time.

Each and every person has some kind of weakness in their body. The number of weaknesses depends on the person, but with one drop of blood an abundance of illnesses can be revealed. Recently I made a measurement with a certain photo that was taken at a medical institution when I was fifty years old, before I became acquainted with waves, and found from the image of one drop of blood thirteen different negative factors.

There were spirits, bacteria, and viruses associated with many negative factors such as rheumatism, diminishing of eyesight, breast cancer, subarachnoid hemorrhage, cerebral infarction, arteriosclerosis, alpha waves, kidneys, edema, constipation, large intestines, cold hands and feet, and breast glands. They were all something that I had experienced. When I was 40 I had surgery for breast cancer, suffered from constipation for 20 years, and also had a hard time from having cold hands and feet. I've had chills go down my spine because I would become sleepy while driving, from a sleep disorder since childhood, and this is from an illness in the brain.

From all the times I took blood samples an analyzed them at 3600 times magnification with the wave measurement

⊖colon (spirit/female) · ⊖thyroid gland (spirit/male) · ⊖arteriosclerosis (5 cells)

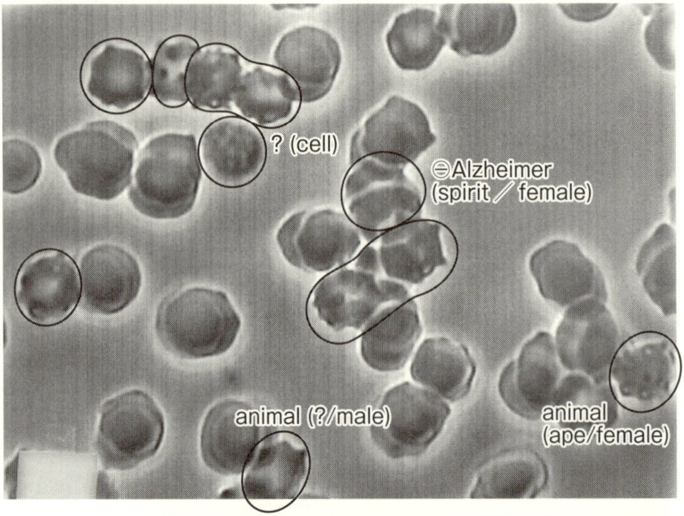

All cells, with many others

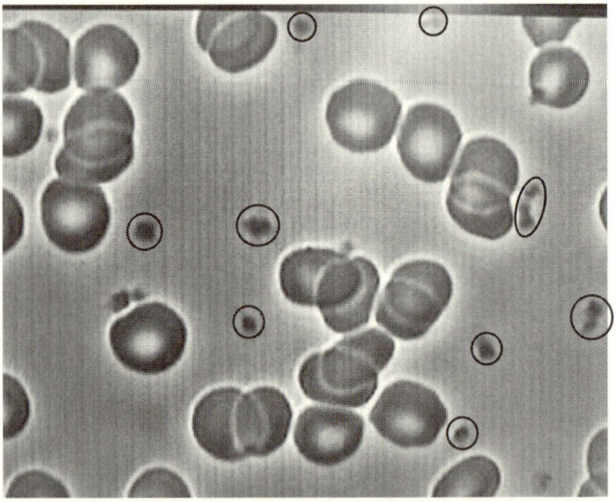

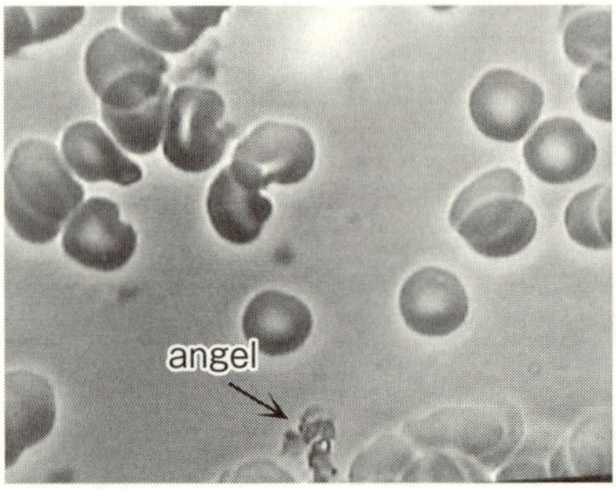

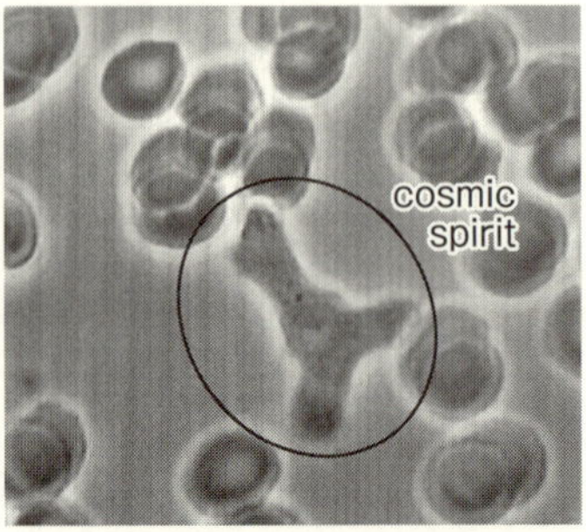

Many jagged viruses with inner ear problems

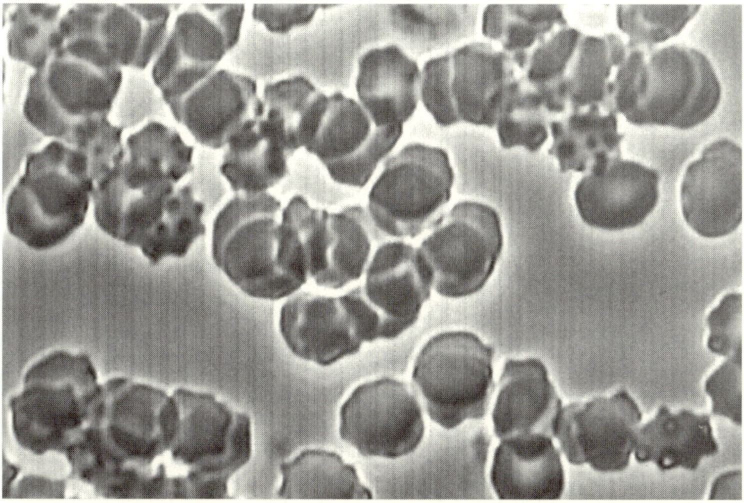

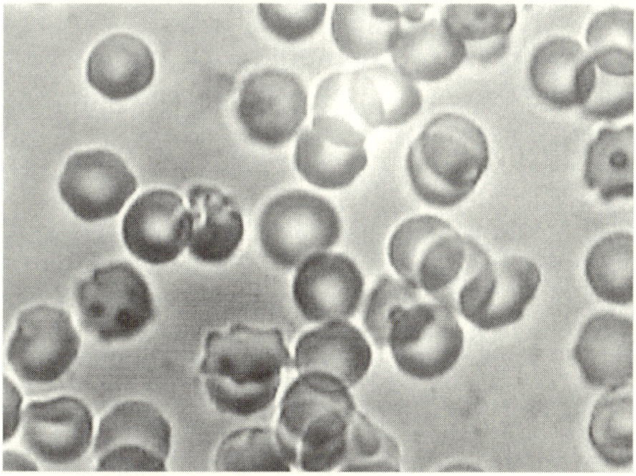

Many various animal spirits

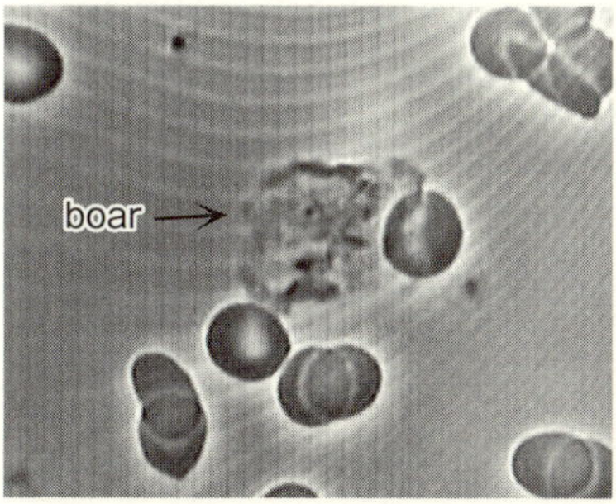

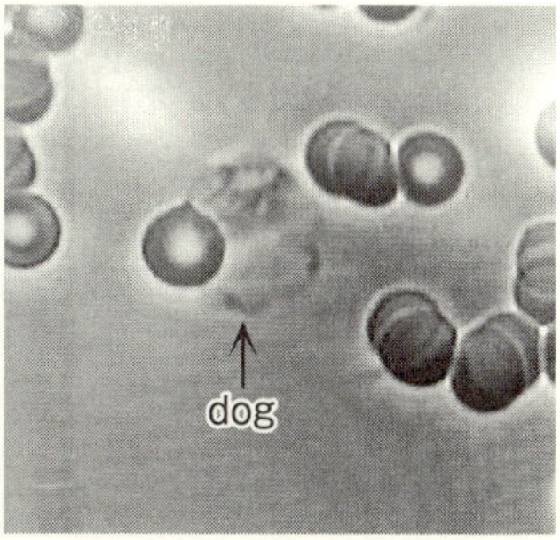

device, the results always matched their chronic conditions. Even though the results may show esophageal cancer, tongue cancer, uterine cancer, Type C Viruses (jaundice), or anything else with no limit, they do not appear in test results at hospitals. A discomfort in the pharynx, fatigue, or the yellowing of hands may be seen as symptoms but the cause unknown.

Purification is done after discerning what negative karma the person has, since the wave measurement device says clearly that bacteria, viruses, and spirits are in fact present. As the purification process progresses, the symptoms become eased, and before you know it you realize that they are gone.

From blood images, you can discover that animal spirits are in possession of some people, and sometimes the image of the animal itself can be clearly seen. Not only snakes, dogs, pigs, and horses, but in unusual cases, there can be pictures, of athlete's foot, parasites, delusional animals, demons, angels, and cosmic spirits. When people are possessed by them they project exactly their personalities and suffer exactly their symptoms.

For example, if you are possessed by a dog, your sense of smell becomes quite heightened. In the case of a pig, the person cannot stop eating and in many cases, is obese. In one certain case, the pig ha a digestive disorder, so the person had stomach pains (refer to Chapter 5 Experiences Having to do with Anybody Being Able to Purge/Bright Yellow Hands/

Unable to Stop Eating Snacks). Personalities and symptoms can occur through the possessed person in this way, also.

Bacteria, viruses, and spirits in the bloodstream will multiply, and with time will harden together. If they contain characteristics of cancer, this will cause cancer, and if they contain characteristics of polyps, they will become a polyp. They can pour out of the body as symptoms as pain, heaviness, numbness, itchiness, or a throb.

As of now Future Waves can find out the exact cause, whether it be genetics, food, pharmaceutical products, health products, or general food products. Any kind of pain or itchiness that has come out from the body can be eased with a Card of Hikari.

Recently the power of the Card of Hikari has become stronger, so purification in to even deeper realms is now possible. Members of the School of Waves take the Card of Hikari seriously, that life depends on it, and keep one at hand wherever they go.

Many illnesses that are given the word "intractable disease"

Patients with intractable disease, all across the world, are suffering without even knowing what is causing it. Every time something like this is shown on television, I take a picture, and make a measurement to discern the cause. I can say with certainty that when the measurement is made, all the causes can be known. This makes me want to tell the person who is suffering about it, and I have sent a letter to several people, but it was no use. The other day, a true story about two people suffering from a developmental disorder was being televised. I immediately made a measurement, and the cause was revealed. One of them was possessed at the forehead by a monkey, an animal spirit that is well known to cause developmental disorders, since being an infant. The number of monkey spirits had been increasing as the baby grew.

The other person was possessed by a bird spirit since childhood. With this person's case also, the number of spirits increased all throughout the child's growth. In this television program there were four famous individuals introduced who were coming out as having developmental disorders. When I made measurements with the photographs of their faces, I saw that they were possessed by bears, snakes, cows, and boars.

There are many people who are possessed by bears, snakes, cows, and boars. There was even a time when my second son was possessed by a horse(male). When we entered his room there was a terrible odor. "What could this smell be?" my husband and I often said to each other.

Eventually, at the age of four, he became sick with Idiopathic thrombocytopenic purpura which is a disease where you cannot stop bleeding. Because it was an official intractable disease of the Ministry of Health, Labor and Welfare, the treatment did not cost anything. However, the condition was serious. He had iron deficiency anemia, B-Type pneumonia, and the value of his GOT (one of the enzymes that produces amino acids) was at 850, with the value for an average person being 50. In was instructed to lie down with his liver spread, and was hospitalized. Mainly there was bleeding from the nose, and when an attempt to cover his nose was made, blood would spurt out from his mouth, and it was often that the room would become a sea of blood.

There was no medicine for this disease, which was a good thing, because then there would be no worry towards side effects. Drugs were prescribed that would make it harder for blood to come out, and also to increase iron, but I threw them away. Because my eldest son had died at the age of one year and one month, I had doubt towards modern medicine. After my eldest son's death I had learned of spiritual healing technique using your hand, and I spent much time with that as my only hope.

It took my second son many years for his GOT value to return to normal, but without drugs he was able to be healthy again. As of now he is quite energetic, but sometimes because of a horse spirit an odor occurs, so I say "something smells" on purpose, and try to get him to remove the spirit by himself. When the removal is done the odor goes away.

Recently, I tried studying the cause of his intractable disease in detail. Not only did I find a horse(male), but a bear(female). I became so surprised that I decided to open his album of his pictures that had been taken since his birth to study them.

What I found was that he had already been possessed by a bear at the age of two weeks. The bear had the qualities of B-Type pneumonia, Idiopathic thrombocytopenic purpura which is a disease, and iron deficiency anemia. My second son had also suffered from atopic dermatitis, and it turned out that the bear was causing that also. From the age of six, a horse came in place of the bear, which caused anemia and negative bromine. As a student he had frequent diarrhea, and in a photo of his from that time, we found an animal, but unsure what kind of animal, that had the negative qualities of diarrhea and bromine.

Just with the three types of animal we were able to know about, my second son suffered from disease. My husband and I don't have any such aspects, so we didn't know why he had them. Nevertheless, the reason why we parent-and-child were sick was because we were possessed by diseased bears and horses. If I had not chosen the path that I am now on, we would still be clueless as to what the intractable diseases are coming from, and would be suffering from it even more.

As a child, my second son had gone near the point of death. I think that his bloodstream was like a wholesaler for intractable disease. With forty years past now, he does not have symptoms or any illness, but traces are still left in his blood.

I myself have experienced this fact, and the people who come to me to consult with also have such experiences. However, the worrisome possibility that an illness may strike again after the process of purification actually does not really ever occur. Purification can also help a person's mood be lifted. The animal that is possessing a person has the same symptoms and the person, so if you purify the animal spirit, both the animal and the person will be purified, which makes the animal happy.

There can be cases where an animal with no particular illness is possessing a person. It is often that the features of that animal are manifested through the performance of an athlete. My second son whom I had been talking about loves to run, and had joined the track and field club, and as he got older became quite an outdoorsman, enjoying sky diving, skiing, and cycling. Looking back, it seems that he had acquired the characteristics of a horse.

Sometimes the aggressive nature of an animal is televised. In a foreign country, there was a case where an elephant went berserk, destroying several cars and a hundred buildings, and was captured. Upon studying a photo of that elephant, I found that the elephant was infested with a virus causing neurological abnormalities. In another case where it was difficult to capture a zebra who had run way, the zebra showed neurological abnormalities similar to the elephant along with anger and fear.

In something else that was televised, there was a blind monkey who was cold, and this made me curious so I went ahead and studied the monkey. There was a female cosmic spirit who had died while having symptoms of glaucoma (an explanation of cosmic spirits will be made in Chapter 2), and regarding symptoms of being cold along with having rheumatism, there was a male cosmic spirit. I felt terrible for them, so I purified them, and the two spirits gracefully went off to the heavens.

A video feed on a television show entitled "A cat fell in love with a stuffed animal! Whose heart was stolen?" showed a male cat walking around with a stuffed tiger from a house next door in its mouth. This cat was possessed by a spirit whose sexual center was negative.

It should also be noted that when a human being is possessed by a spirit, bacteria, or virus which has a negative sexual center, the person loses reason and self-control. There are many celebrities who have committed rape, but pretty much all of them have been possessed by something with a negative sexual center. In the United States, there are horrible stories of parents not being able to restrain themselves, locking their own child in the basement and committing the unthinkable towards them. These acts are criticize quite strongly, but if you were to be possessed anybody would lose reason. Come to think about it, the ones committing the acts themselves are unfortunate.

If there is negativity of the sexual center in the bloodstream, this can be inherited by a child through blood or breast milk. Thinking about this makes me want to purge the world as soon as possible, in fear of what would become of it if it was to not be purified. The things I have been discussing are the root of disease and crime, and instead of thinking that "bad things happen to other people," please understand that it could happen to you, too. However, if spirits, bacteria, and viruses are purified the horrible things can be removed. If everybody understood this and took action toward it, we can solve the problems.

Incredible knowledge that can be attained

Much insight can be attained from images on television.

One time, an abandoned cat was being shown. The abandoned cat, which had become a bit wild, took another abandoned cat under its wings after reaching maturity. Also, a fierce dog whose aggressive nature was uncontrollable, was taught to behave intelligently by this amazing cat in ways that were far from feline.

I assumed that this amazing cat was possessed by a god. In a hurry, I took a photo of the amazing cat to make a measurement, and found that the Kannon-sama was there. I thought to myself at this moment that perhaps this cat can become a human being in its next life. The owner had been taking in an raising stray cats and uncontrollable dogs that were about to be put to sleep, and the Kannon-sama was with this person also.

Here is another story. A male stray cat had fallen in love with a female stray dog and they were sleeping next to each other. The two of them had become close. Eventually, as it became difficult for the female dog to walk due to a brain disease, the male cat helped her walk, nursing her with efficiently. Upon studying the female dog's image, I found that there was a cosmic spirit with cerebral infarction, so I purified it. I hope that his will allow the male cat's nursing to become easier and that the two can enjoy their time together.

From here, I will talk about incredible knowledge that can be attained through wave measurement.

In the past there was a news broadcast saying that several American spies were exchanged for ten Russian spies between their respective governments. There were no pictures of any of the American spies, but the ten Russian spies all had their picture televised, so I made measurements of them and found that there was one animal spirit of a snake, three dog spirits, two obsessive spirits, one resentful spirit, and three cosmic spirits. In terms of personality, four of them were scheming, and six of them were false. This was an interesting case where the spirits possessing them had similar personalities towards these people who were in a special field of work.

There was also a television program that talked about a teenage idol who committed suicide by jumping off a building, with the motive unknown. As I studied the forehead of this individual, the values for depression and stress were at the highest. At the location of the suicide, there were waves of a spirit that had died with depression and stress. The person's body was carried away, but the spirit remained there.

There was a news report of two young children smoking cigarettes. No matter how hard the adults tried to hide the cigarettes, they would find them and smoke them. I studied the children and found cigarette-addicted spirits possessing each of them. The spirits were borrowing the children's bodies in order to smoke.

When there was a news report of a two-year-old who went missing, I made a measurement with the picture and found an obsessive spirit with a delusional an scheming mind. The child was found two kilometers away in a mountain, but a child could not go there by him or herself. What this means is that the spirit took the child there, and this kind of thing happens every day.

It is not only bad things that can be revealed. At the age of ten, Bao Nakajima began writing his thoughts down which eventually became a best-seller with a hundred thousand copies sold. He earned the reputation of a philosopher, but this boy's work was done through the Kannon-sama possessing him, with a goddess giving him dreams and fantasies. He had been receiving their waves.

Mysterious phenomena of creatures can be explained after studying their waves. A huge number of corpses of sardines, dolphins, and whales coming up to a shore is often broadcasted, and each time I have seen it on the news I have found the cause. At some occasions it was a flu, but in most cases cesium radiation could be found in the gills.

One may think of Fukushima when hearing about radiation, but before the disaster of eastern Japan, there was news about herrings being washed ashore in another country that was reported. What this means is that radiation is emitted in to the ocean from a different country, not Japan. Perhaps the people responsible for this occurrence think that radiation will become thinner in the wide space of the ocean?

There was news that the greatest coral reef, 60% of the world, became extinct. I studied the pictures and found many viruses associated with rheumatism. If such photos are taken from all around and they are purified, there is no doubt that the corals with return.

Aside from these particular cases, in Thailand there is an incredible phenomenon where a ball of fire is spat out from water. From a television show that was featuring this phenomenon while trying to unravel its cause, I took four photos and studied them. It turned out that the cause was two spirits of sadness, two spirits of obsession, animal spirits, monkey spirits, spirits of revenge, and two Satanic spirits of falsehood. In a list for the wave measurements, there is a code "Satan 39A1." All spirits that are Satanic are negative in terms of thankfulness, self-centeredness, falsehood, collaboration, and morality.

As the level of wickedness of criminals who are reported increases, there measurement is more negative. However, Satanic spirits, which can be observed quite often, can be measured as negative but the degree does not go as far as causing chaos in society.

Satanic spirits remind me of a baseball player who was televised for having his contract cancelled in 2016. A piece of a bat which had broken came flying and stabbed a player in the leg. I studied the feed and saw that there was a Satanic spirit associated with muscle tissue and scheming. There can be such accidents where spirits are the causal factor. Then they remain and cause more harm.

At a marathon in Hakone there were two brothers trying their best together, an always competing for the 1st and 2nd places. However, in one particular important selective competition, one of the brothers was selected out of the race. When I saw a picture of that event, there was a scheming Satanic spirit who was getting in the way.

There is an example that occurred in my immediate environment. A certain woman who came to consult with me every year always had the same problem, that one of her four children had suffered from an accident and was hospitalized. Upon making a measurement, I saw that all of the four children were possessed by a resentful and selfish spirit.

An enormous accident occurred on April 22nd, 2016 at 4:27pm, the bridge girder of the SHIN-MEISHIN EXPRESSWAY collapsed during construction, leaving two dead and eight wounded. After studying it, I found a Satanic male spirit at the construction site associated with thankfulness, selfishness, and anger. I was afraid of any possible future accidents, so I purified it the next day.

When I was watching a boxing match on television for New Year's eve in 2016, I could not stop myself from studying the match. It wasn't something I had planned, but I found spirits possessing several boxers. There were two who were possessed by angry Satanic spirits, and one who was possessed by an angry, resentful spirit.

I wanted the competitors to fight as equals, so I purified all three spirits. The angry Satanic spirits in particular were dangerously out of control, so I was afraid. Thankfully, though, the boxing match turned out to be good.

Like so, as long as there are images, purification can be done extemporaneously towards a match or tournament to improve its conditions. However, though I notice many people in the crowd who have illnesses, I do not attempt to purify them due to their overwhelming quantity. Not only that, but they would perhaps go back to their doctor who would perceive their better condition as something due to pharmaceutical products or other methods of treatment at that time, and they would be put at risk of entering a vicious cycle where they would be drugged even more than before. With animals, though, they cannot speak of their suffering, so I try to purify them on the spot as much as possible.

The truth which was discovered through the mortuary tablet

On New Years of 2017, three people from Tottori Prefecture came to see me.

One of them had suffered the loss of their eldest son six years before from a death with unknown causes. As a mother she had worked earnestly to ease her sense of unrest, but because there was no proof or evidence of there being anything wrong with her son, so without a pathway she had resorted to seeking consultation numerous times from friends. As an outcome of the consultations, the idea of seeking the answer to the mystery of the death through having a conversation with the deceased occurred, and the friend brought this mother to me.

The story begins with the marriage between the mother's son K and a woman he had met at a singles' party through due to an unexpected pregnancy. K was told by the woman that she had become pregnant, but the number of months of the progression of the pregnancy did not match the amount of time they had been a couple.

Both of them left their parents and began living in an apartment together. Six months later, K was found collapsed at his workplace after eating from the lunch box that his wife had prepared for him. Though an ambulance carried him to a hospital right away, after three hours he was dead. The cause of death was said to be a heart attack. However, suspicion towards his true cause of death arose and K's mother asked for a DNA test. The DNA test was not approved, and she had been searching for a way to solve this case herself ever since.

Pictures of K before he died were sent to me, along with those of his wife, his Buddhist altar, and mortuary tablet. I studied them and found that K was at his mortuary tablet, still left in this world, his soul being negative. Upon measuring his waves, I saw that mercury, harm due to toxicity, and his stomach were negative. I told this to K's mother, who then said that actually bones around his stomach were found to have turned green.

In order to begin purifying his soul immediately, I asked to be sent again a picture of K's mortuary tablet with offerings there. When I studied this picture I did not see K there but a cow instead. The cow was taking the offerings, eating the rice and persimmon, and drinking the water. It seemed that a cow that is not going to its next world was possessing the mortuary tablet. Because of this K was unable to be at his mortuary tablet, and instead was in the corner of his altar.

After explaining that there was a cow, I received the reply that it could be the cow at the house she grew up in which had also given birth. In this other house they also have the altar from their previous house. So the cow from that house could have been here. I purified the cow first, then asked K to return to the mortuary tablet.

After this, the thought that perhaps the discoloring of K's bones could be evidence occurred to me. I asked for pictures of his bones at his grave be taken, and I saw green bones that were negative in terms of mercury, harm from drugging, and the stomach. I also noticed two male spirits who died from lung disease and depression. Upon confirmation with the woman who had consulted me, I saw that the waves of these two spirits showed results that matched their cause of death.

Then, I asked questions directly to the soul. From 2016 I began to be able to have conversations with gods and souls (refer to Chapter 2 Ro-Ne-Ra-Wa-Yu-Wa (Conversations with Gods), and was confident that I could have one with K's soul. I asked the mother to ask her son's soul to come with her to where I am, but when she came his soul was not with her. To solve this problem, I used the picture that was sent to me on previous day to have the soul warp over.

The method to have a conversation is the same whether the other party of the conversation be a god, a soul of a person, spirits, bacteria, viruses, cosmic spirits, or Cell. First the questions are written down, and the answers are also prepared. The spirit will come to the answer that matches. Then I take a picture, and in this case, the answer with the waves of K's soul would be the answer.

I will itemize the answers that came as I proceeded with the questions.

ANSWERS:

"The child is not K's child."

"There was detection of the wife sending pictures of the child to the real father through her cell phone and email."

"After death, a conversation has heard at the wife's house regarding poisoning. The lunch box was not given to (K's) mother, and the room was locked shut in order to hide evidence."

Finally, I asked K: "Now we know the facts. Do you feel that you would like there to be redemption?" The answer to this was "Yes." I followed with the question "Are you happy with the plan that your mother has?" to which the answer was also "Yes," and our conversation ended. From the mortuary tablet we found out that death was due to mercury, and from the bones of the grave we found out mercury was used for intentional poisoning. The truth became revealed. I hope that the case will be solved swiftly.

Conversations with bacteria and viruses are possible

One day, my computer stopped working. Machines are not my forte so I was clueless about how to fix the problem. I was still writing my manuscript, so this was a major disaster for me.

What I did was take a picture of it to see if anything bad is possessing it, and found a Satanic cosmic spirit at the switch. Could this spirit be trying to block our progress? I wondered. I decided to ask God.

What I discovered from the conversation with the cosmic spirit was it could not stand the attitude of A(a manager in a prestigious company)'s attitude. During that time, a large number of cosmic spirits with a potent odor were in the vicinity, so I wondered if A was possessed by a police dog. This came with a strong ability to sense the smell of what was in the environment, with the utterance of "I can't stand this smell!" the colleagues were being purified one by one. When I said, "isn't this a good thing since everybody is being purified?" the cosmic spirit said he was thankful for that, but then went on cursing, saying "That stupid idiot!" with animosity. Her patience had reached a limit.

Until we heard differently from God, we didn't like them, thinking that they were just bad and harmful. The hateful words coming out of her mouth were not usual ones. When asking God about the cosmic spirit, the reply was that the spirit had no evil intentions such as invasion.

Apparently, the intention of the cosmic spirit is to help her friends. All I could do was say "When he comes next time I will inform him of that. Please allow that to be the action for now," and she left to where her friends were. Her strong emotions had made her measurement be that of a Satanic code number. This Satanic cosmic spirit truly loved her friends.

Satanic spirits and cosmic spirits are actually good, and if you just have a conversation with them, even though purification had been difficult, the conversation itself can lead to the decrease in symptoms. This is an amazing fact.

Then I began thinking of how nice it would be if we could purify bacteria and viruses more quickly, and asked God about it. I was told to have conversations with them, also. I was very surprised to hear this, and could not quite believe that bacteria and viruses could understand words. But I felt that I must try to do it because God told me so. I commenced to speak with the bacteria and viruses that were coming out of my body. They understood every word I spoke and gave replies. They gave me the impression of being pure and innocent. When it became time to part, I felt they I want them to stay with me forever, because I grew to like them so much. The reason why they can be simply thankful, I believe, is that when I have them come out of my body, then purify the location where suffering occurred, most of the spirits, bacteria, and viruses all become souls, and the suffering ceases. (With waves also, spirits, bacteria, and viruses come out as being souls.) At that point I said, "You have been taken outside by the light of God, and have been eased of your suffering as well. But if any of you are still suffering, please say so honestly. There are many gods here, and you can be healed. I'm going to ask everyone, so please answer." I created a selection of 4 answers to choose from.

1. **I feel very good.**
2. **I feel so good it's as if I've risen from hell in to paradise.**
3. **I'm still suffering a little.**
4. **I'm suffering at the same level as before, unchanged.**

Thankfully, 99% of the souls choose number 2. They have all passed way before and have been in a state of suffering for decades. I think they were able to be grateful for it in their heart through acceptance. One time, there was the answer that nothing had changed, so I checked, and just as it was pleaded, pain and aching hadn't healed. What could the reason be? Yearning to pursue the answer, I studied this case and saw that the negativity of sexual center, testicles, and pain had not become positive. I asked the soul if they had ever committed rape or any kind of sexual crime, and the answer was "Yes." I

"You are being made to pay in your afterlife for the crime you committed, at a level that is 100 times, which you have experienced as suffering. God's light was allowed to shine on to you as to the others, yet only you were not relieved from suffering. However, you have been honest, and now understand about suffering in the afterlife, so today I will ask God to help with relieving your suffering. Please become a soul that saves others," I said, and helped the soul become positive.

There was also a case where I was unable to sleep until 4 in the morning for two consecutive days. Who could be haunting me? I needed to find the culprit. As the sleep disorder came, I discovered viruses with negative parasympathetic nerves, and had a conversation.

"You have come to me for 2 days. Was there anything you wanted to say?" I asked.

"Yes," was the answer. The virus had notice my previous conversations, and then decided to come. I kept the conversation going, and it turned out that the virus used be a female human being, but became a virus. I asked if the virus had made people reverse their lives in terms of day and night, and the answer to that was also "Yes." The following things were what the virus wanted to say, which made it come to me for 2 days.

1. I am very regretful of what I've done. It was wrong.
2. I would like to come out with this fact.
3. That is one of the things that I can do as of now.

As a result of wrongdoing when the virus was human, its afterlife was affected, the woman's rank falling from human to virus, and was suffering from symptoms similar to its crime in its previous life as punishment, its cycle of day and night being reversed, which is something associated with parasympathetic nerves.

I hope that everybody can go through a similar experience to change their life in a way that would be praised by God.

Japan, the nation of people drugged by pharmaceutical products

Japan is said to be the nation where pharmaceutical products are used the most.

One of the people who attend the School of Waves has been taking medication for 15 years since his 30s. At that time, he was hardly able to get up. Still young in his 40s, without hope or dreams, he suffered obstacles such as anxiety, fear, chills, pain, vomiting, headaches, sleepiness, insomnia, dementia, panic, having residual urine...all of his systems were showing abnormalities.

This person one day at our meeting brought medication to

have them be measured. The amount was overwhelming, so I took just one pill out of the ten pills in nine varieties and pasted them on paper, creating a list, then studied them.

There were 9 types: anti-depressants, anti-panic seizure medication, meds for high cholesterol, meds to soothe panic (2 types), meds for his thyroid gland, high blood pressure, pain relievers, and probiotics.

I found that 7 of these drugs were bad for cerebral infarction, hippocampus, and dementia. Also, it was found that spirits, bacteria, and viruses were include here and there inside the drugs. Those additional aspects were creating new symptoms to arise. Their symptoms matched exactly the symptoms that she was suffering from. We are able to remove these spirits, bacteria, and viruses from the body, which makes us understand very easily their relationship with the drugs. Symptoms can disappear immediately which makes us able to prove this as being true. This is the same not only for members, but any person.

Also, she had become senile, and was unable to go shopping or do her household chores. She says that after beginning to come here, the cause had finally been revealed, and her head is returning normal because of the purification, allowing her to be relieve step by step. Though she had experienced frequent frustration, the cooperation of her family and our faith truly bared fruit.

There was another woman, now in her fifties, who had bad kidneys from age 10 to 17 which lead to nephrosis, and was taking drugs to lower her blood pressure and diuretics. She was a child and was obediently taking drugs recommended by her parents and doctor. However, this caused her to have burns in her stomach, be constipated, and acquire pimples on her face, so she did not want to take them, but took them anyway.

These drugs previously taken sometimes still affect her negatively, and the stomach burns and constipation return, she says.

I've taken her also to where blood samples are tested at 3600 magnification, and a significant amount of the drugs she had taken 30 years before were found there. We also found out why she had nephrosis. There were many male and female cosmic spirits with bad kidneys in her blood. At first it might have been just one spirit, but once a spirit enters the bloodstream, it will desire strongly to escape their trap, and because of this the spirit will expand, multiply, an symptoms will arise. Here the root cause has been found, but if you have the cosmic spirits with diseased kidneys come out of the body and talk to them, along with purifying their kidneys for them, you and they both can be relieved of many years of suffering. We are now able to achieve these results with the power of God.

Drugs, in my opinion, have gone in the wrong direction because of their source of manufacturing is oil. In the previous example where the woman had been using medication for 15 years, apparently she can smell oil during purification when her head feels heavy. The drugs became trapped in the head, and they lowered her brain function over the years. In this modern age, most people take some kind of medication. Because of this, dementia and Alzheimer's are increasing, causing problems at facilities that care for the elderly.

There are many ways that can solve this in a simple way, but what is important is to escape from past traumas, and feel anew.

If there are doctors, hospitals, or any brave people who can take this into perspective, I would like to assist them. My hope is for Japan to become a country without such hazards, and to make this happen collaboratively. We would like to ask for everyone's help.

Chapter 2

Ro-Ne-Ra-Wa-Yu-Wa (Conversations with Gods)

Seoritsuhime-sama

I host a session for the School of Waves twice a month, and there was a session on August 28th, 2013. On that day, somebody said that "There are clouds in the sky towards the west that look like the ascension of a soul.

When I looked, I saw that there was something that resembled a face in the sky. "Could this be a spirit from the purification on that day?" I thought. I took a picture, printed it, saw the ascension taking place on the left and on the right, with an opening in the middle where there was a large face.

When I put the detection rod of the wave measurement device, a high level wave of both man and woman was able to be detected. Also, when I placed a different photo with negative waves, it became positive.

I thought at once of the Kannon-sama, who happens to be both genders and would certainly have higher waves. The Kannaon-sama could have been protectively overseeing our efforts to purify spirits that were possessing people in the School of Waves, and guiding the people who were possessed. Later on we confirmed that the faces were that of Seoritsuhime and the god Taharaketen. It was the first time I had received a message like this in a noticeable way.

Then, in 2015, with the help of God we created the Card of Hikari. At that time we had been using a magnetic necklace that was quite expensive, costing 300000 yen, for purification, To have greater results, we need to have many of them, so wanted to find something that would take its place that would have power. The Card of Hikari has developed to be able to turn anything negative into being positive. In experiments it has proven to be able to purify radiation, which was like a dream come true. It all came about from meeting God.

At that time, though God was present, I was unable to have a direct conversation. However, because I was able to talk to the soul of my cat Musashi who died at the end of 2015, I had also become able to talk to my ancestors (Chapter 4 The Afterlife) which made me think that conversations with God would also be possible.

Upon thinking, there were two pictures with terrible waves that nobody could purify, so I set them next to each other. Then, I wrote down the question "Is there a god present with high waves?" along with "yes" and "no" for answers and have the god come there. This would mean that the waves of the picture with the answer "yes" would be purified and turn positive.

After trying this, I measured the waves of the picture with the answer "yes," and saw that indeed the waves had become positive. The god had truly come! I was delighted that I was able to contact a god. After the god arrives, the rest is simple. Yu can measure the waves of that god, so even if someone else answer, you can just say that you will ask the god the question.

During one of my first attempts, even though I was asking a question to a god, other evil spirits facetiously answered instead. Afterwards, they were munching on the rice which had been put aside as an offering (not for them of course). This made me angry, and I shouted, "I'm trying to ask a question to a god, and not only are you interfering, but you are eating the offering for the god! Would you lie to be burned, drowned, or salted as or punishment!?"

I had left the front door open, which allowed many wandering spirits to enter. I was careful after that episode. I purified these evil spirits with salt for one week.

I then went ahead and asked gods questions. Out of the many questions that were asked, I will make a list some "yes" answers.

"The publication of the book is important. Tell the truth."

"God's light is infinite, and can purify radiation and nuclear weapons."

"The cause of a lot of earthquakes is angry animal spirits."

"The reason why the Kannon-sama came to my house is because my love towards nature, Earth, and animals is similar to that of the Kannon-sama."

"Your actions affect your degree of happiness in your next life."

"This life is the astral world."

"People who commit wrongdoings suffer in the afterworld accordingly."

"Hell, as depicted in Buddhism, exists."

"The Sanzu River exists."

"Promises about how one's life will be are made before one's life begins."

"Usually death awaits when one fulfills their purpose in life. My son, who died at age 13 months, was born with that purpose."

"The karma of my son being born as my grandchild 42 years after his death (Chapter 4 The Afterlife, My child who was born after 42 years!) came to be because his soul is the one that will fulfill the inheritance of Future Waves."

"People who have a god at their forehead are in that situation due to the number of times they have reincarnated or their events in their past life. The way of thinking and personality of that person comes from the god."

"The reason I have been able to come this far is because I have been guided by God while putting my effort and passion for the pursuit of knowledge in to my work."

During that time, I had been giving thanks and asking for guidance from God on the 1st of each month. On June 1st 2016 I prayed again, but as I gave an apology from being unable to meet the wishes of God, I felt something welling up inside of me that was not my own, but someone else's mind.

Then, as I began to cry, I thought that it could be the Kannon-sama who was causing the forming of the tears.

When I asked later, I found out that this was true. I asked for an official name, and the answer was "Kanzeon Bosatsu." The official name is somewhat longer, so upon attaining permission I began to refer to this god as "Kannon-sama." There was a shrine in my house, but nothing set up for Kannon-sama, so I asked a question.

"Would it be better if there was a shrine for you, Kannon-sama?"

"If possible, yes."

I knew which room and what location to have the shrine, but I had no idea what type or shape it should be. What I did was write down some names of people who were knowledgeable about gods, and a circle was formed around the name of Houkan Togari, who had retired from work at a temple and was studying the roots of gods.

I had known his sister. Kannon-sama told me to ask him through her, so I asked her and she agreed that we go to Kyoto together. We took pictures of household shrines together, and Kannon-sama picked. Whenever there is something I do not know, I seek the answer in this way, which helps me not be burdened by wondering which is the correct answer.

Houkan Togari inherited his father's temple, but presently his son is in charge of it. At the sister's house, a drawing of

Kannon-sama made by Houkan Togari was on the wall. To me it looked as valuable as a national treasure, and being struck by it I asked him to please draw one for me as well.

Ever since, I have become friends with Houkan sensei, and on August 29th, when he came to my house, he said "Let's ask for the name of the Kannon-sama," so we decided to have a conversation. Kannon-sama was both a god and a goddess, and the name of the goddess was "Seoritsuhime." We asked where she was from, but perhaps the question was not purposeful enough, because we could not get a reply. It became late so we finished.

On that day, we looked up Seoritsuhime-sama on the internet, and there was an explanation that she had married Amaterasuoomikami-sama. I saw how gallantly they were portrayed in an image, and I became humbled that I was associated with them.

Afterwards, going through the Japanese alphabet one by one, I asked for the name of the god, and it turned out to be "Tahatarateken" which took 2 hours to figure out. We were then taught by the god that this name is not known in the world.

Both the god an goddess that are Kannon-sama have gone through reincarnation 20 times or more. As it is explained in Chapter 1, when there is a god at a person's forehead, the waves of Kannon-sama that are both male and female, a symbolic feature for this god, can be confirmed. What it is that the god has a male aspect and female aspect, and the two share common will as one god.

Both Seoritsuhime-sama and Tahatarateken-sama were involved in the creation of Japan according to legend, and I asked if most of the legend was true. They both give the same answer, which moves me emotionally that they share the same thoughts.

Answers

"Amaterasuoomikami-sama is actually male."

"The true form of Amaterasu is a male god which leads to Amateru and Nigihayahi."

"It was a different god that was actually in the story of the Iwato-biraki."

"It is true that the world was create with Japan as its model."

"The story that 16 princes were sent out to the world to create nations is also true."

"The excavation of items with the emblem of a chrysanthemum, which is the symbol of the Japanese imperial family, happening around the world is proof."

"Extraterrestrials come from planets such as Saturn, Pleiades, and the Big Dipper."

On October 19th 2016, I decided that I would like to ask questions to Kannaon-sama who had been with me for nearly 70 years. I hadn't had any conversation with this god yet. To avoid confusion, this Kannon-sama is the one who has guided me and watched over me for a long time. The Kannon-sama who I talked about previously (Seoritsuhime-sama and Tahataraketen-sama) came to my house later and supports the role I play.

The Kannon-sama that I am more personally connected to dwells in my forehead, but when questions are asked, yes and no answers are given from outside the forehead.

Question

"I ask the Kannon-sama who has been with me since childhood. My grandson who has now been born has had the same Kannon-sama with him in his past life. Was the Kannon-sama with me also guiding me in my own past life?"

Answer

"Not in your past life."

"Your purpose has been decided at the time of your birth."

"Your path was set up for you to meet this purpose."

"There was meaning in the day of your birth and 33 strokes (from "happy fortunetelling for birthdays")

"The death of your child was part of the design for you to meet your purpose."

Question

"I heard that I was born with a purpose. Did you know that the work with waves would develop this far, and that it would allow me to make discoveries?"

Answer

"The ability grew during the course of events."

"Your pursuit of knowledge bared fruit."

Question

"Where was I able to gain the confidence to be given such an important purpose?"

Answer

"You were diligently working to discover things in your past life."

"Your love towards nature, Earth, and animals is strong."

"Your sense of justice is strong, which makes you want to defeat evil."

"You have a soul which has always wished for world peace."

Question

"Does God know the future?"

Answer

"The future is already decided."

"However, the future can be changed."

"God's power and mind helps move things in a positive direction."

I had been thinking about nuclear weapons, so I had the Kannon-sama who I have been talking with (Seoritsuhime-sama, Tahatarake-sama) join the conversation and asked them.

Question

"Currently, nations of the world are making statements and

taking actions for their own benefits. Is this what brings about war and destruction?"

Answer

"Yes." (Answered by four gods.)

"There is the threat of nuclear weapons, and the danger of the end of humanity." (Answered by four gods.)

"It wouldn't erase the entire human race, but those who would be left would be in a world of suffering."

"Things are getting dangerous, so there must be collaboration for the sake of preventing it."

In the beginning of 2015, the Card of Hikari was made with the help of God, but Kannon-sama eventually told me to remake it. Distracted from my busy life, when I was feeling a bit of ease from my schedule, I made a decision on November 3rd 2016 to make a new one. I asked for help from Kannon-sama, who took my request pleasantly, and an amazing, big light was entered in it.

God's light can heal humans, animals, plants, Earth, and all of the universe. The Kanzeon Bosatsu also says that the Card should be used for people with true faith, thankfulness, or love towards people, animals, and the planet.

In this modern age most people cannot believe in such things. Without some kind of proof, words alone cannot permeate through the heart. I used to be one of these people. Even when being taught by an educated person, I could not believe. However, my eldest son died at the age of thirteen months, and I had breast cancer, and my second son caught an intractable disease, and after all the crises that I had gone through I finally met waves. Now I know that there is a reason to everything, for example disease, personalities, earthquakes, war, and all other phenomena. There is evidence to prove all of it. I attained this truth through the power of God, and my confidence has grown strong.

Your behavior before life becomes reflected in your afterlife

About a year passed since May 2016 when I became able to have conversations

with gods.

In my daily routine, anything that I don't understand, I ask gods for answers.

From February 2017, two more gods began staying at my house, making four the total.

This god is also male and female, reincarnated more than 20 times, but they were not married. Apparently they are unable to decide their birthplace, and according to their purpose they are born in various countries. So I wrote down 16 nations that I could think of, asked all the gods if they've been born in any of them.

Tahataraketen-sama had been born in America and Saudi

Arabia, Seoritsuhime-sama had been born in France an Saudi Arabia, and as for the other two, the female had been born in China and Iran, and the male had been born in Cambodia and Iran. The last country was the same, and there they had built rapport, and now they were fulfilling a mission together in Japan now as one god.

A I've mentioned earlier, two gods have been with me since I've been born, but recently, two more have come so now there are four. I asked why, and the answer was that they've been watching me purifying, and that they are in my favor, and decided to come help me spread God's light to the world. Now there were four gods with me, and together with the four gods in my house, there was a total of 8 gods.

Three members of my School of Waves said that due to karma with Okazaki, gods came to them also. Gods coming to help is the most precious form of assistance, so there is much to be thankful about. Also, I gained information from a member about a You Tube video about researchers who investigate UFOs, and from that video I measured 35 people, researchers, professors, and celebrities with their images, an found that gods were possessing all of them. There is no falseness in these kinds of people. Just like us, they say that the universe belongs to everybody, so we must protect it.

At this point, I asked the gods about things that were in my mind.

Question

"There have been about ten people that I have met who have not returned money that they owe me, or have not paid for a necklace. What will happen to them?"

Answer

"They will experience suffering that will be 100 times worse."

"They will be dropped in to a world of darkness."

"They will be born as subhuman creatures."

Even if you feel that you profited in this world, you only live about 80 years. I hear that the afterworld is 500 to 1000 years. When I became married, I lived in Aichi, and at first I had only 500 yen to last me an entire week. My husband had quit his day job, and the business that he had started was in the red. During that time, a certain friend sent me 500000 yen and told me that I don't need to return it. When I became able to return the money, I returned it at about twice the amount. With thankfulness you can return somebody's generosity.

My life changed 27 years ago. When preparing for my lunchbox before going to work, I always used silver paper to separate the food. At that time there was no okazu-ire to separate the rice from the other food. We were in the age where Apollo had landed on the moon, but somehow there was no okazu-ire. I thought that people were in need of it, so I decided to create a product. Me, a housewife who had never been involved with manufacturing or sales, went to take on the manufacturing of a lunchbox that is completely sealed without leakage, a very difficult thing to do. It was a reckless thing to do.

At first there were no sales, and challenges took a stronger hold day by day, but the idea of the product grew, and it became a hit. Other ideas also became hits. I have been on television three times as "the idea housewife."

However, when something becomes a hit, false versions of it are made. There are corrupt enterprises that make defective ones. When defective versions are sent in to the market, what was once a hit will no longer be, so you must create a new product. This made me restless with worry. However, because I was blessed with an able husband, I was able to manage it.

When I began, I always prayed to God that my products would be a hit, that if I became wealthy, I would serve the world. The first idea that I had, the lunchbox, something that I was confident about, was shown to me when I woke up in the morning. Looking back, I feel that God had truly shown me the way.

The purification of spirit-groups

Conversations with gods always was one-way, with me asking questions. It occurred to me that gods may have certain things on their mind that they want to talk about as well, so on April 4th, 2017 I asked 49 gods.

Question

"I have a question for you. May I ask each morning whether you have something to tell me?"

Answer

"I believe that is a good idea."

Question

"Is there anything you wish to tell me today?"

Answer

"Yes, there is."

I wrote down various things on a piece of paper, and the words chosen were "spirit" and "good."

Answer

"Your spirit is fundamentally good, but there is a group of spirits who are at work against you."

"Your problem is the group of spirits, and no one can exorcise them. You must think of a way now."

"If you are going to take action, sooner is better."

"There are several countries affected by the spirit-group. This includes North Korea, China, America, Russia, and Korea."

Question

"Should I purify the spirit-group when I find them?"

Answer

"Yes."

The opportunity came right after two days.

On April 6th America fired 59 missiles at Syria, and there was disorder in the air. Furthermore, there were 33 Satanic spirits near the ship that was relate to the missiles fired by North Korea, along with 3 spirits around the face of the top, one near a building, and one around the American president, making a total of 38 spirits.

I am always removing spirits from bodies, but this time I was worried because there were so many Satanic spirits gathering somewhere outside. Thoughts like "Should I purify them little by little?" or "Should I purify them outdoors?" came to me with fear, but all 55 gods said that I must talk to them.

I made a decision, and called all 38 spirits to my room. If you call a spirit, they will warp over and it doesn't even take a minute. This time, as usual, I called the spirits from afar. We started the conversation after the purification.

Question

"How do you feel, mentally and physically?"

Answer

"Like having risen from hell to heaven." (all 38 spirits)

Question

"Why were you all having the thoughts you were having before?"

Answer

"We were being brainwashed." (all 38 spirits)

Thirty-five spirits were from North Korea, and 3 were from South Korea. They had never been overseas, and not being told current events of the world, they were just following commands faithfully from their superiors. I will not get in to detail in this book, but they knew the culprit behind the murder of the brother of Kim Jung-eun.

I had 35 of the spirits stay overnight, and the following morning I had them listen to the news about North Korea. They seemed to not know why North Korea was under pressure from other nations. At the end I asked a this question.

Question

"Can all of you go back and stop the provocations by Kim Jung-eun?"

Answer

"We will strive for it." (all 38 spirits)

Then on April 7th at 1:39pm, the 38 spirits went back to their home country. I reported what happened to 80 gods.

"The reading of the measurement came out as Satanic, but the spirits were just brainwashed. They were pure but unfortunately abused. I am glad that I was able to help North Korea and the spirit-group even a little, with the help of God. I was so thankful that I began to cry. Thank you so much."

Afterwards, I studied the video of the United Nations

Security Council from the news, and saw 402 Satanic cosmic spirits behind the right side of the conference hall. I also discovered that behind the left side there were about 20 gods.

The next day, April 8th, I witnessed a spirit-group spread out all over the world, which made me afraid. I asked a god what I should do, and the god answered "There is no need to worry. All of their souls are pure," which gave me courage.

The day before, in the School of Waves, I had spoken about this subject and there were people who wanted to participate in the conversation because it was such a rare opportunity. I talked about people wanting to participate in the conversation with the god, and we began it as scheduled on Monday.

Monday morning came. There were now 500 gods. Because there were 402 spirits, the number of gods was also great, and I felt overwhelmed.

Question

"There seem to be a great number of gods. Is it for assistance?"

Answer

"Because it is a precious occasion." (all 500 gods)

Question

"I would like to begin. All of the spirits at the United Nations Security Council seem to be female, but is this correct?"

Answer

"There is no need to worry, please proceed as usual."

When I counted the number of gods then, there was nearly a thousand. I exchanged glances with the other people who had come, wondering what was going on. There were so many that even the gods themselves were surprised. I called the 402 spirits with no worry. We began the conversation after 30 minutes of purification. The conversation was long, so I will summarize it.

Question

"I would like to ask how everybody feels."

Answer

"It feels so good that it is like rising to heaven from hell. When alive, There were hard times and a sense of defeat. After hearing from you, now there is a sense of hope."

Answer

"We are 368 spirits from Iraq who were killed by an attack by America, along with 34 spirits from Turkey. We were angry towards America, and wanted revenge."

They all stayed the night, and I read out excerpts from the manuscript. They gave the following answers.

Answer

"We were moved emotionally. It's mysterious, but because we are souls we understand very well. We wish this had occurred when we were alive. Hopefully people all over the world will read it."

Answer

"So glad to be here. We are also glad to have been able to meet with gods. We were so moved by it. Thank you so much. We will now go on with the things we have to do."

After parting ways, I gave a report to the gods.

"I was stunned by the number of gods that were present, and it made me realize how important the occasion was. I had hope that effort would prevail, but they were not what I had imagined to be, and it made me realize why the gods were recommending the conversation. Before, when I had measured waves as being Satanic, it made me think of evil only, but now my perspective has changed so that I can see that they have suffered to the point of becoming Satanic and that I must recue them at once. I hope that there will be no victims like them in the world. And it has been confirmed inside me that the best way is to tell people there is an unseen reality. This too is because of the conversations with you gods. Thank you very much."

When I sais this, there were answers from 2411 gods, which means there was an increase of 1000 gods. I asked a question immediately.

Question

"Where have you come from?"

Answer

"From overseas."

Back during a time when there were less than 50 gods, they were from Aichi prefecture. When there were many cosmic spirits, the God of the universe was also present. I thought that there were participants from overseas because I had been working with global affairs.

Later, amidst the civil war of Syria, there was a report that the Asaad regime had used Sarin, a toxic chemical weapon. When I took the picture of the place where the chemical weapon was used, there were 46 spirits with neurological abnormalities. I called them to talk to them, and found out that they were killed in the war. While feeling fear from the bombings, they kept on living there. The fear towards the bombings apparently have not stopped even after their death. No wonder they have stress and neurological abnormalities. They were victims of war.

The purification of Plutonium

Looking at current trends, it seems that there is so much tension that war could break out any time.

On April 12th 2017, the gods told me something harsh, and I wept in tears from sadness and disappointment.

Answer

"War will occur."

"It can also be stopped."

"God cannot take measures directly."

"Human beings must take care of themselves."

"The only way is to purify people and spirit-groups."

From this conversation, I realized that things would go too far if nuclear missiles were fired. The other day I had purified radiations from North Korea, which made me think that I could find it this time too, so I studied the satellite images, strengthening the Card of Hikari, taking time off from volleyball which I love.

I was able to find it easily, but what I found was a great amount of radiation and plutonium. Before, at most there was only ten, but this time there was 100 times the amount. It was night, so I inquired to gods the next morning.

Question

"I found a lot of radiation and plutonium in North Korea. Shall I purify it?"

Answer

"It's better for plutonium an radiation to be of no use."

"The radiation inside the missile can become harmless."

"All you have to do is purify it."

"Just do what you always do."

Radiation an plutonium are not souls, so I purified them

outside.

“Thank you God, I have now purified them, and they have disappeared in to the sky.”

Answer

“The danger of radiation from North Korea is now gone.”

“Electric power using radiation should stop being used in the future.”

“The electric power technology that we are participating in now is the best.”

Question

“Otherwise, should I deal with spirit-groups when I happen to find them?”

Answer

“There’s something abetting the American President.”

“You will find out more when you have a conversation.”

This was the answer of 3500 gods. And again, from the internet, I found pictures of Satanic spirits, spirits who are self-centered, stressed out spirits, bacteria, viruses, and purified them. Also, I called spirits that were possessing Kim Jong-un and his subjects and purified them. After having the conversation, I sent them home. There were cosmic spirits a lot of the time.

There was worry that a missile would be shot on the birthday of Kim Il Sung, but it didn’t happen, which was a relief. The number of gods in my house increased day by day, and on

April 16th the number had reached 10000. They were all in the living room, but it was cramped, and I was worried that they were put at an inconvenience, or that others would be unable to come because of lack of space.

More than 37000 gods of the world!

On April 16th, I finished writing Chapter 2 Ro-Ne-Ra-Wa-Yu-Wa (Conversations with God) The Purification of Spirit-Groups, so I asked about how the manuscript was, and how I should proceed hereon.

Answer

"It is very well done." (20488 gods)

Question

"I wondered if it was all right. Thank you very much. In the world of gods, is there anything being worried about?"

Answer

"We want war, pollution, and over-medication to end."

Question

"There are a lot of gods present, but is this an anomaly?"

Answer

"These occasions occur from time to time. Gods have a network. This particular gathering is a joyous occasion.

The following is from a conversation on April 17th.

Question

"North Korea seems to have failed its missile test. Last time, after purifying, they failed three times. Did the failure happen due to the purification?"

Answer

"Yes. It also involves purifying spirit-groups and publishing the book."

Question

"The number of gods is now over 28000. With this great number perhaps there is not enough room, so why not use the tatami room, reception room, and the second floor?"

Answer

"The tatami room is preferable."

Question

"Will the futon be suitable?"

Answer

"Yes that'll be fine."

I prepared 2 and a half, but the next morning there was an addition of 5000, so I prepared another one. It became April 19th, and one of the members of the school of waves had a temperature of 40 degrees. I received a notice about it, that although the purification that was done for 5 minutes helped the fever to calm down, there still was coughing, so attention was needed. After making a measurement, I found cosmic spirits. Recently, it seems that cosmic spirits are in possession of many people, including myself, those around me, and criminals on the news. I asked the gods what the reason and background of this is.

Answer

"The cosmic spirits have come from various planets as souls."

"They come to be friends and to cure illnesses."

"When cosmic spirits come to Earth and eat what people and animals are eating, they will enter the body of people and animals."

"Currently a great number of cosmic spirits are inside the bodies of people and animals."

"Most people don't realize it, but they are everywhere."

"Use the Card of Hikari and purify."

The number of gods at this time was 37000, so I added another futon.

Question

"The world is in a state of tension. Will everything be all right?"

Answer

"There is a spirit-group affecting Russia."

I studied images from the internet, and found 9 Satanic angry negative male spirits in England, and 7 saddened spirits on the waters in Russia. They were cosmic spirits.

Answer

"Go ahead and purify, then have a conversation with them. We are also concerned with the 9 Satanic spirits." (32240 gods)

On Monday April 24th, I called the 9 angry Satanic spirits in England and the 7 saddened spirits in Russia. I began the conversation with them after purifying for more than 30 minutes.

Question

"Thank you for coming all the way to Japan. How do you feel?"

Answer

"It feels as if we ascended to heaven from hell." (all 16 spirits)

The 9 angry spirits had originally come from within the galaxy to Vietnam on Earth. However, they lost their homes during the Vietnam war, and were being angry in England. Their planet has water, vegetation, and air, but their technological advancement is not as progressed, and they don't have automobiles, airplanes, or hospitals. The 7 saddened spirits were victims in Iraq during the Gulf War, and they were cosmic spirits. Three of them were born in Iraq, and 4 of them were born elsewhere in the Middle East. It is strange that descendants of extraterrestrials would be born in the Middle East, but I heard from gods that back when a spaceship from Mercury crashed in the Middle East, the Mercurians that survived married local people, so this is understandable (Chapter 2 Ro-Ne-Ra-Wa-Yu-Wa).

All of the 16 spirits were victims of war also. The 9 spirits in England were still angry, even as spirits, that their homes were taken away. This makes me remember the 46 spirits who suffered stress from neurological abnormalities due to the chemical attack in Syria. War destroys crops and buildings, making people, animals, plants, and even souls in a different world angry. A tragic chain reaction occurs from the anger and sadness that it causes. It has to stop.

"Light from the East": this means the light of God

On April 27th, I took my camera and went outside to bring in the soul of my cat Musashi. The thought occurred to me that perhaps the existence of gods could be observed from outside the house, so I took a picture of the entire house.

I found 21880 gods from the picture. The next morning, the measurement I made from inside the house was a match, which made me realize that I could measure from outside as well. During the peak, it seemed that 37000 gods were all going back to their areas. While there were still many, I asked about the soul along with questions that other members wanted to ask.

Questions

"Currently, using the light of God, I am taking out spirits, bacteria, viruses, and cosmic spirits from the bodies of people and animals. What happens if they remain in the corpse?"

Answer

"Sometimes they can escape, but not usually."

"Souls that cannot escape are doomed to perish."

"The spirit of a deceased comes out of a body after one to two hours."

"Souls are given birth to in the spiritual world with the light and consciousness of God."

"God had something to do with the creation of the universe and everything in it."

"God had given many people this message before, but there had not been any proof or exactitude."

"And now we are using modern equipment, so there is much to be expected from this first occasion of being able to have conversations with gods. Equipment is being used, and there had better not be any mistakes misbeliefs."

"We expect great outcomes from being able to use one photo to purify."

Question

"Gods from all over the world are present, so I will ask. There are different religions at war against each other, but this is wrong, isn't it?"

Answer

"Yes. God is the same everywhere in the world. There are no differences in true religion. People are using religions to benefit themselves."

Answer

"War is being used by people."

Answer

"Radicals who speak of a holy war are mostly brainwashed youths."

Answer

"God wishes for the world to stop war, pollution, and destruction and become a world of love."

Question

"There is a tradition that 'light from the East.' Am I correct to interpret this as modern equipment and the light of God coming together in the East (Japan) and being sent out to the world?"

Answer

"Yes. The future had been known."

Question

"In this chapter, there is information about the 16 princes who were sent out to the world to create nations (written later). If it can be confirmed that the ancestors of all tribes lead to the same, that would be marvelous."

Answer

"Yes, that is true."

In the four-hour conversation, 19992 gods gave answers.

On April 30th, more gods had gone back to their country. The next day would be May 1st, and I thought that more would go home, which made me hurry to ask more questions.

Question

"During the past year I have verified that the Card of Hikari can purify radiation, and is the greatest tool. Members of the School of Waves depend on it. However, there were people who could not understand it, be thankful for it, or see the depth of its capability. What can I do to spread it?"

Answer

"Decide the price of the Car of Light. Make it 100000 yen. It should be the same around the world. The size should not only be L, but also name card size."

I understood. If it was free or cheap, it would get thrown away. I don't want something that I value to be treated that way. A person willing to put that much in to the purchase would certainly take care of it. It would give me funds for my activities, so I felt that it would be two birds with one stone. What I can do in return is to tell people about what I learned from gods. There were 8045 gods this day.

The evening of May 1st, most of the gods had gone home, and there were only 746 gods. In April more than 37000 gods had come to stay in my house that was not very spacious for them. On the 13th, with the purification of plutonium and radiation of North Korea, the number of gods increased, and by the evening of the 15th there were 200000 gods. On the 17th there were 30000 gods in the living room, shrine, and on top of the refrigerator. They must have been cramped. On the 17th, with delay I recommended they use the other rooms, and I was filled with regret that I was not able to notice that they had been feeling cramped sooner.

The other regret I have is regarding their food offerings. Meat and fish are not allowed, but eggs are okay so I made rice bowls with eggs, but found out that none of them had eaten it. The next day, I made curry with no meat, but it was the same result. I felt so bad about it, especially because they had come from afar.

I looked at what they were eating every day and gained the following information. I found out after about two weeks, but many of them had gone back to their countries. Thoughts of regret cross my mind all the time.

Christ, Mohammed, and the Buddha

On May 3rd, 2017, as a continuation of the other day, I asked about religions.

Question

"How are the saints, Christ, Mohammed (Muhammed), Buddha, and John, who spread the central religions of the world, doing now?

Answer

"The other day, when the gods of the world had assembled here, they were also present, and now Christ, Mohammed, and Buddha are still here."

Hearing that these great people that are known all over the world made me feel so moved that my jaw dropped.

Question

"Have these three been reincarnated after they passed away?"

Answer

"Not since their previous life. Before becoming a saint, they reincarnated dozens of times. It has been a few thousand years, but they have been watching over people from a heavenly world."

Question

"A person who has studied the Bible would like to ask about the Old Testament and New Testament."

Answer

"The Old Testament is a collection of stories made by people. The New Testament is partially true, but some of it is false."

"God's name being Jehova is true."

"There is a story that Jesus will defeat Satan's world and create the Kingdom of God, but people should work at it themselves, and not rely on God."

These answers were given by Jesus.

Iron Balls Falling

It was May 14th, 2017, a day that I held a meeting for the School of Waves, which I do twice a month.

In the morning I was vacuuming in the hallway. From above, brown iron balls the size of pachinko balls made noises and came rolling. Did a part of some machine come off? I looked around, but there were no machines or their parts. I wondered if it could be a god, so I asked.

Then I got that answer that there was meaning in dropping the iron balls while I was cleaning. I asked if the iron balls had anything to do with a war in some country, and I was right. It was not America, North Korea, Russia, or China, but a different country.

It became my task to purify the President. The god selected the alphabets one by one for the name of the country. As I searched for the President on the internet, members belonging to the School of Waves gathered.

One woman said "Suddenly iron balls came falling, but

where did they come from?" and was looking around while holding them. I realized that the ones I had put on my desk were gone, so I explained the situation to her. She was quite knowledgeable about gods, so they must have wanted to communicate to her as well.

The President of this particular nation was possessed by spirits with neurological abnormalities or those that were self-centered, so I purified. However, when I asked if everything was all right, the answer was that there were more. After the session for the School of Waves, I studied the President meticulously, and found three cosmic spirits that were negative in terms of falsehood, anger, collaboration, and thankfulness, so I purified them.

Afterwards, I asked more questions regarding religion.

Question

"Are there others besides Christ, Mohammed, and Buddha? If you could give me specific names, I think that it would help people understand that true religion is one."

Answer

"Yes, that is a good idea."

Koutama Okada of Mahikari and Daisaku Ikeda of Soukagakkai were present. I had once learned a great deal from the Mahikari religion. I feel that their teachings have helped me progress to the level that I am at now. I felt doubt towards the soul of Daisuke Ikeda, so the next day I asked. It turned out that it was not a god but a normal soul. It was a spirit suffering from paranoia because of medication for neurological disorder.

The god then said that lies will eventually be exposed, and said it with emotion. I spent an entire day purifying the paranoid spirit. This helped calm his nerves, and I again began the conversation.

Question

"You have been purified with the light of God. Yesterday you claimed to be Daisaku Ikeda. Are you able to understand that you are not him today?"

Answer

"My head is clear now. It was as if I wasn't myself."

"I respected Daisuke Ikeda greatly. I had neurological sickness and was taking medication at a hospital. I followed someone here."

It became clear to me that symptoms during life can affect one's afterlife. I was able to prevent it this time, but if such a spirit was to possess a person, then the possessed person would also have those symptoms, and they would have to go to the hospital. On the news, phantom killers and violent crime are reported, and what I've found is that almost all of them are possessed by spirits with neurological disorder. There are many cases where people suffer from such spirits even though they are not reported on the news. I hope that people find out about the root cause of these things and learn to deal with it properly.

Regarding the sixteen princes

On May 18th, 2017, because I had asked Koutama Okada questions and he had answered that the teachings of Mahikari are mostly correct, I took out one of its old books, and asked questions with "◎absolutely correct," "○correct," "△somewhat," and "×wrong" as possibilities for answers. A lot of the answers came out as not being "absolutely correct."

Although I myself have trouble finding answers, the gods simultaneously an decisively give the answer. All of the answers were quite understandable. In one of the sections of the book, there was something about the sixteen princes, so I asked questions after reading aloud the following:

"Before the Jinmu Emperor, there was a vast history with the Tenjin Nanasei, an imperial lineage of 25 generations, and the Hukiaezu seventy-three generations. The origin of the history of humanity started with the emergence of the five major ethnicities during the reign of the second emperor. However, natural disasters divided the land in to various nations, and the sixteen princes of the second emperor, the ancestral origin of the five ethnicities, were sent out to strengthen the divisions of the five ethnicities. These 16 princes were sent out from the

Spiritual Origin (Japan) to be kings of 16 nations, and spread teachings. A great amount of labor was required to teach the doctrines for those nations.

With the 16 princes there became 16 positions, and a divine symbol was created where there is a circle in the middle (the God of Creation) and 16 lines with a hewn chrysanthemum. This became the original form of the symbol, and it is related to the symbol with the 16 chrysanthemums on the shoes and sword of Tutankhamun that was buried in the Pyramid, along with a similar symbol engraved on the Unopened Door of Jerusalem. Other similar discoveries are also evidence. What this means is that long ago, we were all one household, with harmonious order without war or disease. The world was a family. This is represented in the Bible as the Garden of Eden or paradise." (quote from Mahikari text)

Question

"Is what I read out aloud just now correct?"

Answer

"Absolutely."

"The names of absolute God are the following. Christianity: Jehova, YHVH (Yahweh). Buddhism: Seikannon (Buddha). Shinto: Amaterasuhiokami. Judaism: YHVH (Moses). Islam: Allah (Mohammed). Hinduism: gods are the same."

"They are all the same God, all absolute, just called by different names. They can also be referred to as the Master God."

This was the answer of 58 gods. Jesus, Buddha, Mohammed, Joseph Smith (the founder of Mormonism), and Koutama Okada were some of them. They were grieved that people were manipulating the names of God that all represent the same God. They had gathered so that this message can be sent to the world.

On May 19th, from conversations with gods, I found out that God is an organization of gods, like a pyramid, with the absolute God of the Universe (and the names that represent this God) at the top. If compared to a government, the roles would be similar to Prime Minister, Minister, Representative, and such.

On this day, I asked the name of the gods who are in this world. They were only names left on a list that was recorded. From overseas, there was the god of the Pygmy tribe (hunter-gatherers that live in a tropical rainforest near the equator in Africa), the god of the Guarani tribe (one of the American aboriginal tribes), and the Rumanian god came forth. There were also prominent gods from Japan. Because the gods were so high-ranking, I was filled with doubt.

Ashinadakakami the sister of Okuninushi

The Amidasanminorikyodan

Amenoikutama

Amenoshitatsukurashishi Okuninushi

Amenohideri Takehiratorinomikoto

Amenohohinomikoto

Amenominukanushi

Kamimusubi Creator deity

Kinooya Sugiharanookami

Kintobi / Kinshi

Daikokuten

Seoritsuhime

Takamimusubi Creator deity

Takeminakatanomikotohikogamiwake

Ninigi Inaho god, god of agriculture, the grandson of Amaterasuoomikami

Hayachine Okami

Wakafutsunushi

There was an interesting episode a few days later on May 23rd. Around 7 am, I had a dream before waking up. Outside the front door there was a figure like Daikoku-sama, with a bag on his left shoulder and carrying another bag in his right arm, standing and wanting to be let in. I woke up instantly, went downstairs, took a picture of the genkan entrance, then opened the door. I saw three gods after measuring the photograph. When I asked a question, a surprising answer came.

Answer

"Daikoku-sama was the one who came."

"Of the three, two of them had been here before, and one of

them was the God of the Universe and it was the first time. The two gods were guides."

I understood that gods would go home when they had things to do, or go meet others, and that that was the reason why their number varied depending on the day.

The legend of Yamato no Orochi and Susano-onomikoto-sama

On May 26th, as I studied the names of other gods, I asked for more names:

Susano-o-nomikoto, brother of Amaterasuoomikami
Kushinadahime, wife of Susano-o-nomikoto
Yashimanunomikoto, first son of Susano-o-nomikoto
Itakerunomikoto, brother of Susano-o-nomikoto
Ooyatsuhime, child of Susano-o-nomikoto
Nigihayahinomikoto, fifth son of Susano-o-nomikoto
Mikashigihime (wife of Nigihayahinomikoto)
Kuraimitamanomikoto
Okuninushinomikoto, descendent of Susano-o-nomikoto
Amanokayamanomikoto
The Jimmu Emperor (the eleventh emperor)

The gods of Japan certainly had pedigree. Also, famous founders of religions had also been present.

Shinran Shonin
Rennyo Shonin
Kukai
Saicho
Ippen Shounin
Ebisuten (2 gods) of Kongokai Mandara
Dainichinyorai (center)
Kongoharamitsu Bodhisattva
Houharamitsu Bodhisattva
Noriharamitsu Bodhisattva
Katsumaharamitsu Bodhisattva
Ashukunyorai
Kongousatta
Kongo-o Bodhisattva
Kongoai Bodhisattva
Kongoki Bodhisattva
Houshonyorai
Kongohou Bodhisattva
Kongoko Bodhisattva
Kongodo Bodhisattva
Kongosho Bodhisattva

Next, from Hokekyou Mandara

Seikanzeon Bodhisattva
Monjyu Bodhisattva
Jizou Bohisattva
Fudo Myo-o
Kongoyasha Myo-o
Aizen Myo-o
Bonten
Rashoumonten (2 gods)
Kongorikishi
Daikokuten

Fifteen from Kongokai and 11 from Houkekai are neither male nor female, and either Nyorai, Bodhisattva, Myouo, or Ten who have not been born human. Also there were living gods who laid the foundation for the modern world, and they are the Richu Emperoror (17th generation), the Hanzei Emperor (18th generation), the Ingyou Emperor (19th generation), Kinashi-sama the eldest son of Ingyou Emperor, third son Yasuhiko Emperor, 5th son Hatsuse-sama, and Komuhachimukamukimu-sama, making a total of 7 gods.

These are gods that worked hard to create the greatest nation of the universe and for the sake of spiritual growth of humankind. Because they care about people and Earth, they cannot rest in paradise, and must be worried about tensions in international relations. Gods seem to be attending United Nations Security Council meetings and G7 summits.

They are saying that Earth has the greatest water, air, oceans, mountains, trees, and animals in the universe. The will of God to protect this planet comes across clearly. Gods who participated in the creation of the universe and this planet all understand the process of everything.

I also asked regarding the civilization of Atlantis and the continent of Mu. Mu apparently was in existence in the past, but the reason of its disappearance is still a mystery. I think the mystery can be solved by continuing the trial-and-error process of questioning gods.

On May 31st, Susano-o-sama was present, so I asked about legends. I had the questions answered as either true or false.

Answer

False: "You were responsible for the Amenoiwato incident."

False: "You were exiled to the Nation of Ne (Nenokuni)."

True: "You slayed Yamata no Orochi in Izumoguni and saved Kushinadaime."

False: "You attained a sword from the tail of Yamata no Orochi and offered it to Amaterasuoomikami."

True: "You are a harmonious god of agriculture who spread afforestation, taking gold, silver, and wood back to Shiragi."

The truth was very different from the image of the legendary juvenile delinquent. He had devoted himself to his country even before birth. And now, with his family, he is working for the future of the planet.

Amaterasuoomikami-sama

On June 6th, a change occurred at my house, where until then there had usually been about 200 gods.

At my house, there is a shrine and a miniature shrine for Kannon-sama adjacent to each other. To find out the number of gods present, I either get information from those two shrines, ask in a conversation, or discern it from images taken from outside. There are various methods. During this time I had been busy and wasn't able to find the number of gods, but on this day I studied the shrine, and saw that there was one god only.

In May when I changed the shrine to something not as hot, I had placed a talisman just for Amaterasuoomikami-sama. There were so many gods before, but now only one, so I asked:

Question

"Could you perhaps be Amaterasuoomikami-sama?"

Answer

"Yes."

I was speechless, and did not know what to do. While being dumbfounded, I asked, "I am not confident that I could be useful, but I will keep the plan going. I would like to ask the names of gods and write them down. Would that be all right?" The answer was "Yes, that would be fine."

Afterwards, I wanted to know when the highest of gods had arrived, so I checked the file I had been keeping of the pictures that I have been taking daily.

Around the end of February there were nearly 100 gods in the shrine and the miniature one for Kannon-sama. But somehow on April 20th there were 24 gods in the shrine and 9 gods in the miniature shrine. On May 1st there were no gods in the shrine and 6 gods in the miniature shrine. The other gods were on the sofa. On May 18th there was just one god in the shrine (Amaterasuoomikami-sama) and 6 gods in the miniature shrine (Seoritsuhime, Susano-o-nomikoto, Kamimusubi god, Fumifuso-o-wahatsuwane, Okuninushinomikoto, Niniginomikoto).

In April, gods from around the world had been here, tens of thousands of them, but the number of gods in the shrine and miniature shrine had decreased. Could it have been to respect the gods who were nation-creators? In May, there still were 6 prominent gods in the miniature shrine who had created Earth. Other gods had moved to the chair from the shrine, waiting to welcome Amaterasuoomikami-sama who would come on the 18th. It had been decided in the world of gods that Amaterasuoomikami-sama would arrive in May.

Who would believe that the divine creators of the universe

and the planet would come to a common home? I think God knows that I love Earth more than anyone, and that I can have conversations with gods.

Though great saints have been brought to Earth, the current situation of the world is unpardonable. With worry that another world war could break out, the gods had decided that it would be good to send out the light and words of God. This has been confirmed through conversation.

God has great hope towards the publication of this book. I was told that if this book is published, a strong collaborator will emerge. The message that "the root of all religions is one" is strong, and founders of religions have also gathered. The founders feel a great desire to send the message that if the top person of religions let go of their ego. With thousands of years passed, they are earnest to communicate this. I believe that people who want to fulfill the will of God will appear.

Thirty-seven gods (a genealogy of gods, 17 gods and 20 living gods)

I will give the names of the gods who I haven't written down yet. These are the names in a genealogy, 17 gods and 20 living gods.

Hayaakitsuhikonokami

Kayanohimekami

Kanayamahikonokami

Kanayamabimenokami

Sokotsuwatatsuminokami

Uhatsuwatatsuminokami

Amenofutodamanomikoto

Hirukokami

Yorozuhatatoyoakitsuhimenomikoto

Futsunushinokami

Taketamayoihimenomikoto

Amenohohinomikoto

Ichikishimahimenomikoto

Isotakerunomikoto

Sarumenokimi

Hosuserinomikoto

Amenokaguyamanomikoto

The following are living gods.

Ankan Emperor (the 27th emperor)

Uesugi Kenshin (the battle of Kawanakajima)

Oishi Yoshio (head officer of Akohan)

Ono-no-Takamura

Kammu Emperor (the 50th emperor)

Kikuchi Takeshige (central figure of the Kyushu

Nancho forces)
Kusunoki Masatsura
Kurozumi Munetada (the Kurozumi religion) a living god of the sun
Sakanouenokaritamaro
Sakanouenokaritamaro no Kisaki
Ookunitoyotinusinomikoto (Shimazu Yoshihisa)
Umedake raishin (Tachibana Dousetsu)
Suigyoku raishin (Tachibana Gintyo)
Togo Heihachiro (Navy military personnel)
Saneyasu Sinno (Ameya)
Hiedanoare
Fujiwaranotokihira
Fujiwaranomorokata
Minamotonoyoshiie
Minamotonoyorimitsu

Before birth they worked hard for their country, and now they are concerned about the fate of Japan and the world. Finally they have found a way to communicate the feelings of God, and have come with great expectations. I myself am worried about whether I can complete my own important task. The gods say that this is the only way, so there is no choice. I share God's mindset of wanting there to be love and peace in the world.

The legend of the Inaba Rabbit and Okuninushiookami-sama

When I asked Susano-o-sama about the slaying of Yamatanoorochi, I found out that half of the story was false. I knew that Okuninushisama was present, so I decided to confirm about the legend of the Inaba Rabbit (Inaba no Shirousagi) as well.

This story is famous. I asked Okuninushisama the questions on June 14th. The answers come as either true or false.

Answer

False: The Inaba Rabbit was skinned because it lied to the shark when crossing the river.

False: While crying from pain, the older brothers of Okuninushiokami passed by and said to wash with sea water and dry in the sun, which made the pain worse.

True: Okuninushikamisama, the little brother, came and heard the explanation, and he said to wash with fresh water and use ear of the reed mace.

False: The rabbit was angered by the older brothers, and tattletaled the truth to Yagamihime.

True: Yagamihime chose Okuninushiokami, the little brother, for marriage.

True: The white rabbit had only been injured.

Okunushikamisama's wife was present, and I received this answer directly from her.

True: She was drawn by the heart of Okuninushisama and chose him to be her husband.

I asked if it would be all right to reveal the truth about the legend in the book, and the two of them said "yes." It seems that what wins over a woman's heart is love and kindness, and that this goes for any time period. After an endless amount of time, they are now beside each other walking the path towards the same goal.

To be completely guide by God

On June 14th, since I had wanted to renew my shrine I had, I decided to take action about it. There are usually about 200 gods there, and there is not enough space.

Previously, I had brought somebody to renew the Kamidana but this person's way did not match what was required by the gods, so I asked the gods if they knew anybody who would be suitable for the renewal, and 232 gods said they did. There was a god protecting people in the city of Nishio, near the city of Okazaki, and this god knew who would be suitable. From the conversation I found out the address.

When I heard that the city was Nishio, I remembered something. When I was contemplating about the shrine, at night I had a dream about a woman name K that I knew who once lived there. I hadn't seen her in 30 years, but K lived in Nishio. I told the gods that I had a dream about her, and asked if K had anything to do with the present task. They said that she did, and that I should go visit her. I departed at once.

When I went to the address, there was a fine-looking mansion with amazing statues of Hotei. However, there was no nameplate or address number, but just the word "A-gumi" engraved in a large stone. I worried if I had come to the right place, and decided to call K who I saw in the dream, but she wasn't home.

I was able to see her house, so that day I went home. I reported to the gods, and was told that the mansion was the correct location, except that I should go there with K. In the evening I called K again, and we agreed to meet the next day. When I saw her, for the first time in 30 years, I asked about the mansion and she said she knows very well about the mansion since it is near her parents' home. She was nice enough to pleasantly agree to go to the mansion together, after listening to my strange story.

When we arrived, the wife was watering the flowers. She allowed us to enter the room, and I explained myself. I worried that I would sound unbelievable, but she said that she was the believing type, which was a relief. During our conversation she called her husband, and a plan was formed for who would be the one to renew the shrine and what it would look like I invite him to look at the location in my house where the shrine will be placed.

God guided everything perfectly from place, the dream, the acquaintance, to the couple that were suitable for discussing the matter. When I reported to the gods at home, I found out that a god had been with me when I met K and the people at the mansion. Apparently the people at the mansion were decedents of gods. I was filled with joy and was given confidence with a sense of certainty from thankfully being able to meet understanding people.

I knew that a god from nearby had been present, so I asked if there were other gods present from nearby locations. I was then told that a god had come from each of the cities of Anjyo, Hekinan, Toyohashi, Chiryu, and Nagoya.

Cosmic spirits and their increase

June 24th. Recently, the usual number of gods is 224, but the day before 7 gods were not there, so I wondered if they had gone back to where they come from.

A little before 5 am, there was a small sound which I identified as the door bell, which made me wake up and wonder who could be at the door so early. It occurred to me that it could be a god, like the other time, so I went down the stairs, took a picture of the genkan, and opened the door. I was still sleepy, so after that I went back upstairs to sleep. When I woke up at my usual time, I looked at the picture wondering what the doorbell could have been, and saw 7 gods.

I asked the gods about this, and it turned out that the 7 gods that came in the morning were the gods that had left before, and now they have returned. The gods come and go freely, but sometimes they give a signal like in this case. I thought that perhaps the sound of the doorbell was made small so as not to wake the other gods, and that it would only be me who would hear it. Amaterasuoomikami-sama was here, and apparently went to investigate.

It is my daily routine to purify spirits, talk to them, then have them go on their way.

Recently, I mostly encounter cosmic spirits. Why are there so many of them? As I asked the gods, light has finally begun being shed on the matter. I even have asked about it to a cosmic spirit.

First of all, the reason is that Earth looks very attractive compared to other planets, since it is the most well-made planet, according to the gods. Teleportation is not possible when alive, but once you are a spirit you can, so many cosmic spirits come to Earth for vacation. However, the fun lasts only for about a week, and what awaits is the worst form of hell. I asked the gods why, and it turned out to be because they get thirsty and drink the water and eat the food that are around. When animals and people have whatever the spirits had, the cosmic spirits will end up entering the bloodstream of that animal or person. Whatever illness, mental or physical, that the spirit has will be transferred. The spirits are trapped until the animal or person dies. Inside the darkness of the bloodstream, wherever they turn there is a wall, they look frantically for an exit. Not only that, but the pain and suffering they had while alive will haunt them. If they stay in the body for some decades, the pain will multiply. This remarkable phenomenon causes conditions to worsen, which is usually thought as being caused by ageing. Even with myself, what used to come out were bacteria, viruses, and spirits, but now all cosmic spirits. I am able to purify faster than others, so I work on it daily, but the cosmic spirits never cease.

If there was one cosmic spirit per person, with 7 billion people there would be 7 billion spirits. There were more than 100 spirits that came out of people that come here, my grandson, and myself. When I start doing the math in my head, it makes me sigh. God is also concerned about this reality. When I found out about this, I became filled with worry.

Many cosmic spirits have mental and physical illness. There is no medicine to help.

The other day, I had the cosmic spirit who was possessing a

cancer patient who had been broadcasted on television, and listened to it. The spirit's suffering increases when anticancer drugs are used. But the person was still alive. I called the spirit from Tokyo to my place in Aichi, and talked to it while curing the cancer that was causing it to suffer. Spirits become quite thankful when they are able to come out of the body they are trapped in and go from being in hell to being in heaven. There is no hell such as this in this world, but the spirits all answer my questions for me because they had been suffering for decades. Before they depart, I always ask them to spread the word about the truth. The cosmic spirit with the cancer said it felt much better after being cured, and went on home.

Spirits are unaware that they can fall in to the hell of being trapped in the bodies of people and animals if they drink water and eat food. This situation is continuing, and will grow, and will eventually become out of control. It is not just Japan, but everywhere in the world.

How did this situation evolve without knowing about it? I think it is because I haven't been able to have conversations with gods or spirits.

I talked about spirits inside the bodies of others, but they can also be inside of electric appliances. When they are next to or on the appliance, turning it on will cause them to be sucked inside. The other day, the weight scale broke, an when I took a look, there was a male cosmic spirit and a female cosmic spirit. I brought them out and asked why they couldn't get out, and they just said that it was impossible. The weight scale now works properly.

When possessed, people and animals get sick, and things and electric appliances will malfunction. The spirits that are trapped may get burned along with the people or things and their soul may become extinct, and if they are buried, they will have to stay there for hundreds of years.

Nobody has any idea about this cruel situation. I finally came to this answer after 17 years of research and talking with gods, purifying with the light of God. With this new knowledge, perhaps we can all work together to not allow this situation to grow any bigger, and if the situation arises, it would be better to purify as soon as possible. That would be progress towards happiness in society.

Chapter 3

A Dream Story and the Unknown World

How a god entered in to my dream which then came true

I forget most of my dreams, but the dream I had on February 10th 2017 was very real, not to mention that it happened right before I woke up. I wondered if a god had sent me the dream, so I asked the gods if they knew anything about it. The answer came from a goddess who was not at my house. The content of the dream mostly matched, and it seemed that she had come wanting to communicate something. There was only one person that I knew in the place that I dreamt about, so I called and explained about the dream. This person then said that it could be an acquaintance. I then confirmed with the goddess that the dream was about this acquaintance.

It was regarding the soul of this acquaintance in the universe, and that there was a problem which needed to be solved. The person I knew agreed to talk to her acquaintance. Through this, I saw the goddess go to work to solve the problem which moved my heart.

Oftentimes, when somebody has a wish and it doesn't come true, they selfishly deny the existence of God, but I feel that when a person's wish isn't fulfilled, it must be because they are lacking in their own personal effort, or that their wish itself is not virtuous, or that there must be atonement. These things probably matter.

The bond between cosmic spirits and anacondas

On July 4th 2017, Typhoon 3 had come ashore, and the Tokai region was in its predicted course. Around this time there were many typhoons, and I was looking in to the matter of there being spirits inside the typhoon, which causes there to be more damages.

So I looked to see who was in the typhoon. There was a snake in throbbing pain from burns. It died in great pain from the heat and burns, so perhaps it wanted rain. However, I have a great phobia towards snakes. Even if it is small, I run next door squealing. Bears and boars are cute, but when it comes to snakes, I flip the photo the other way when I make the measurement.

I had asked the gods the other day if it would be safe to call the snake, and the reply was that there was no need for worry, which was encouraging. So I gathered my courage together and called the snake that was in the typhoon.

Question

"You seem to have throbbing pain from burns, but how are you?"

Answer

"It still hurts."

Question

"I will make you feel better gradually. What caused your

burns?"

Answer

"It was caused by the burning of dead grass in a field. I wanted water desperately, so I often went to where there is rain or a typhoon, and if I go in to a rage, the rain and wind sometimes become stronger."

I purified it as we had the conversation, and later it went off without any pain. It was due to the selfish behavior of people, that the burning took place while the snake was resting, and it probably had no escape and died. It was a pity that the throbbing pain still was there even after death.

Afterwards, I called those who I was instructed by the gods to purify. Under Baghdadi in the Islamic group, there was a female with neurological abnormalities, and a Satanic male and female who were in the force.

Those who were able to come out of the bodies had been experiencing hell for a long time, so they were thankful to be released. I had once thought that spirits were the ones causing disease and bad personalities, but actually the spirits had fallen in to a state of hell. The spirit who entered the body and the actual owner of the body both were in pain.

I talked to them so they won't experience hell any more, and asked them to spread the word. They went off. All three of them had rice with beans before leaving. I'm sure this will ameliorate the minds of Baghdadi and the people in the force .

Once I found out that the snake wasn't scary, I started wondering about other snakes. Then I discovered a male and female panic-stricken and awfully stressed snake in the world's weather radar over Australia. I was concerned so I called them.

I listened to them, and it turned out that they were married. The wife ate a panic-stricken animal and also became panic-stricken. The husband was nursing her and became stressed. Then as I healed them and talked to them, they said that they felt better, and that they would like to spread the word about the good things they heard, and off they went. Gods told me later that they were spirits of an anaconda couple.

As this was going on, there was news that North Korea fired another missile. I was frustrated and resentful that in my busy schedule something like this would come up. In the previous missile launch, there were numerical readings of radiation, and when I purified it, the launch failed. It seems that in recent launches they do not include devices with radiation. When I measured the face of elated Kim Jong-un, I saw that there was a female cosmic spirit with neurological abnormalities hovering over him. I called her to the house.

Otherwise, there were 26 cosmic spirits around Saudi Arabia, so I called them and talked to them, and it turned out that they had been to my house regarding the United Nations Security Council in April. (refer to Chapter 2 Ro-Ne-Ra-Wa-Yu-Wa (Conversations with Gods) the purification of spirit-groups) But if my memory served correct, there were 402 cosmic spirits at that time...

I asked what happened to the other 376, and they answered that they went back to Mercury. Later, the cosmic spirit who had been hovering over Kim Jong-un and the 26 cosmic spirits said that they would like to stay the night, so they ate, and I made a place for them to rest with towels.

The next morning I told the 26 cosmic spirits that I would like to call the others, and they said they'd be happy if they could come. I asked the 376 what Mercury is like.

Answer

"It is more advanced than Earth."

"There is a mountain of things on Earth that are not on Mercury."

"There are just as many creatures in the ocean."

"There is order in the environment and maintenance."

"There are no conflicts like war that there are on Earth."

"Vehicles similar to cars fly and move about in the air."

"There is electric power available anywhere."

"There are train tracks and transportation occurs at high speed."

"There is an agriculture and fishing industry."

"There are hospitals, too."

"Life is easier on Mercury than Earth."

The woman who had been with Kim Jong-un and the other 26 cosmic spirits listened with me. I then asked them:

Question

"After hearing this, did you think it would be better to live on Mercury?"

Answer

"Yes, we want to live on Mercury."

Question

"Why don't you all go live there?"

Answer

"Yes, we will."

Question

"This is a question for those who came from Mercury. Is there anything else you would like to communicate?"

Answer

"We want to show the advancement of Mercury. It is a good place."

Then they all went back to Mercury. How nice it would be to hear about the progress of Mercury again, and the reasons why there are no wars, so that we can learn from it.

On July 7th, there was report of a massive rainfall that left damages in Kyushu after the typhoon left. I took a look, and there was a male snake and female snake, so I called them.

They were siblings, and according to the sister, the brother would go to where there is rain when he starts to panic. The brother said that the rain would ease his tension.

Question

"There is heavy rain in Kyushu now, but can you take the rainclouds over to the ocean?"

Answer

"Yes we can." (brother and sister)

Question

"Can you take the giant typhoon-like thing to the ocean as well?"

Answer

"There will be need for more of us, but it can be done." (brother)

"There are snakes with ability and snakes without ability." (sister)

Question

"Thank you. It was good to be able to talk to you. When the typhoon comes, I will heal the one who is sick with the help of God, so could you snakes move the wind and rain to where it would not cause harm?"

Answer

"Yes." (sister)

"I can tell the others to come together." (brother)

Question

"How big are you?"

Answer

"We are quite big."

Question

"Do animals have anything to do with earthquakes?"

Answer

"Yes they do." (sister)

"When our anger becomes explosive, we can make earthquakes happen as well." (brother)

I asked them to help with the heavy rain in Kyushu, and to assist in the future when a similar thing happens. Then they left for Kyushu. Later, I looked at satellite images of Kyushu, and saw the snake siblings doing their best there.

I was worried that Kyushu was too large of an area for just the two of them to handle. I also saw that there was an unpurified cow and a cosmic spirit there. I didn't want them to get in the way of the snakes, so I called them over.

I also called over the Anaconda couple who had left on July 4th, and asked them all questions.

Question

"The heavy rain in Kyushu is worrisome. I asked two snakes today to handle it, but are there any among you who could send the rainclouds to the sea?"

Answer

"We can't." (cow and cosmic spirit)

"We can." (anaconda couple)

Question

(asking the anacondas) "Do you know how to get to Kyushu?"

Answer

"Yes." (wife)

"I can go help." (husband)

Question

"Is your panic better now?"

Answer

"It is cured."

Question

"How big are you?"

Answer

"We are big snakes." (husband and wife)

I asked the anacondas to go help the snake siblings, and to assist in future typhoons, and had them go after a meal. Apparently the cow had passed away from not being fed.

There are many earthquakes in Kyushu recently. During the Kumamoto earthquake I was glued to the television, purifying the various spirits and animal spirits I saw. At that time I was not able to have conversations. I just purified the spirits that were there with light and sent them to the heavens, so I don't know if they have been relieved from their pain and suffering. I would have to call them over and ask each of them. I hope that I will be able to someday.

This time it was the anaconda couple that I called over and talked with, but with all the ones I have conversations with, I feel that we become best friends. It seems that I have more of these friends than living ones. Later, I confirmed with the weather satellite that the snake siblings and snake couple were working in Kyushu. They are conscientious and nice, which makes me glad.

On July 8th I found a male snake with bad prostate in Russia. I was concerned about it so I called him over. As I purified him his prostate condition improved.

Question

"How do you feel?"

Answer

"I feel great." (anaconda who had the prostate problem)

Question

"How big is your body?"

Answer

"I am a big snake." (anaconda who had the prostate problem)

Question

"Can you move rain and typhoons?"

Answer

"I can move big ones if I have others to help me do it." (anaconda who had the prostate problem)

Question

"Is your prostate better?"

Answer

"Yes, much better." (anaconda who had the prostate problem)

Question

"I'd like to call over the 4 snakes who have been working hard to get rid of rain clouds. Would that be all right?"

Answer

"That'll be fine." (anaconda who had the prostate problem)

Question

(questioning everybody together) "Yesterday morning you snake siblings went to Kyushu, then after 4:30 in the afternoon you two married snakes (anacondas) also went. I saw that you were working very hard. Thank you very much."

Answer

"The clouds divided in to 2 parts, and the clouds above the archipelago have begun to go away. The 4 of us worked on it." (anaconda husband and snake sister)

Answer

"We were able get much of the rainclouds towards the sea, so the worst part seems to be over." (snake brother, anaconda wife)

Question

"How do you feel about moving rainclouds?"

Answer

"It would be tiring to do it every day, but sometimes would be fun." (anaconda couple and snake siblings)

"It is an easy job." (anaconda who had the prostate problem)

Question

"The worst seems to be over in Kyushu."

Answer

"We will finish so that the weather will be clear." (anaconda husband, snake brother)

"If there is lack of rain, we can cause rain to occur as well." (anaconda wife, snake sister)

The anaconda with the prostate problem agreed to assist from hereon, so I thanked all 5 of them, and they went off after having a meal. This was the day before the session for the School of Waves, and as I talked about this episode to the person who had come to help for it in the evening, I decided to ask the gods about the anacondas. The answers came from the 239 gods that were there that day.

Question

"Dear gods, thank you always. I've asked some snakes to calm a heavy rainfall in Kyushu from yesterday. Five of them were here today. They all said that they are big snakes. What does that mean?"

Answer

"They are anacondas."

"The couple who had suffered from panic, and the one who had the prostate problem are anacondas."

Question

"Was it a good idea to ask the anacondas to calm the heavy rain?"

Answer

"Yes."

Question

"What about asking dragon gods or dragons?"

Answer

"Dragons are also good."

Question

"I saw a dragon bigger than the entire archipelago of Japan. Could I ask this dragon for assistance as well?"

Answer

"Yes you can."

"You can ask for help when there is an emergency."

Question

"The dragon bigger than Japan didn't seem to have a spinal cord. Was it a cosmic dragon?"

Answer

"Yes, a cosmic dragon."

Question

"I can ask a cosmic dragon for assistance?"

Answer

"Yes, you can."

On July 13th, the archipelago had no clouds above it, and as I looked to see the five anacondas, I just saw that there were the two anaconda siblings there, and that the others had gone back to where they had come from.

I looked further back in time, and the 5 of them were all above the archipelago by 7 pm on the 12th, and then went home after confirming that the rain was gone. They worked hard for 6 days, from daytime on the 7th until the 12th, so I felt that I should call them over to thank them some time soon. All animals have a heart and a conscience, so I hope that people will treat animals well with respect.

The anaconda which became reunited with its family

On July 14th, I decided to take a look at anacondas from around the world.

Actually, with the wave measurement device, big snakes can be measured as "snake," but somehow anacondas are different from snakes, and the device responds towards them only with waves that are human. Anacondas must be at a high spiritual level.

Because they are enormous, any satellite image will capture them, making them easy to find. On this day I found 2 anacondas in the west of Africa, so I called them over.

As I listened to them, I discovered that they were mother and son. Both of them had died of disease, but the husband had been taken away by people, and they did not know whether he was dead or alive. The son died because of his bladder, and he said that there still is something wrong with the bladder, so I purified it while I talked to him. He said he felt better.

I talked to them about what happened during the heavy rain in Kyushu. I remembered that the anaconda who had the prostate problem had also helped, so I asked them a question.

Question

"How was your husband's prostate?"

Answer

"It had a problem. Maybe that was my husband." (mother)

"I want to find out." (son)

It hard was hard for me to believe this coincidence, but I thought that it would be nice to have the anacondas get together, since I hadn't properly thanked that anaconda for the other day. I called him over immediately.

Question

"Thank for the other day when you worked very hard to move the rain in Kyushu. Today there are 2 anacondas here who are mother and son. Do you have any relations with them?"

"They are my wife and son." (the anaconda who had the prostate problem)

"He is my husband/father." (wife anaconda, son anaconda)

An unbelievable wondrous family reunion happened.

Answer

"This is the greatest happiness ever. We are moved to tears." (whole family)

The father went back to their home to live after being killed by humans, but could not see his wife and son because they had moved to Africa. The mother and son had been waiting for a long time for the return of the father, but it had taken too long, so they had given up and decided to move.

Question

"How was the moving of the rainclouds in Kyushu?"

Answer

"It was easy." (the anaconda who had the prostate problem)

Question

"It took many days, but were you able to have a meal during the process?"

Answer

"I was doing it without any meals." (the anaconda who had the prostate problem)

Question

"If there is any trouble in the future I would like to ask for your assistance again."

Answer

"Okay." (whole family)

I had always been offering an egg that was still inside its shell, but nobody would eat it, so this time I cracked it open and offered the inside, and everybody ate it.

I always open the front door and take a picture to make sure that my guests have left. So this time as usual I took a picture, and was surprised when I was going through my pictures the next day. There was a gallant image of the face of an anaconda in the sky. A person who happened to be present said that it was a dragon. The face in the sky had the waves of the anaconda family. The next day I investigated where they gone to, and the place was in Africa, where the wife and son had been.

There is more to this story.

I found out later that the Phoenix had appeared in the photo that was taken when the anaconda family departed. On October 28th, 2017, I called the Phoenix and asked some questions.

Question

"Are you the Phoenix who appeared on July 14th on the day of the reunion of the anaconda family, along with 3 gods and 3 goddesses?

Answer

"Yes."

Question

"What brought you here on that day?" (I asked this and some other questions.)

Answer

"We came to bless the reunion of the anaconda family."

"There are other phoenixes as well."

"The appearance of the Phoenix according to the legend in China is incorrect."

"The role that the Phoenix plays is to be a symbol of peace, and to appear when something occurs that leads to happiness."

"The Phoenix has reincarnated several times like gods and dragon gods. The order is to be a peacock, then a phoenix."

"The Phoenix is also known as Fushicho."

On this day I found out that the Phoenix is not the same as the god in the legend.

Others who happened to be present and I are very emotionally moved to discover these new things by coming in to contact with gods who live in the world of dreams that we read about in legends such as Amaterasuoomikami-sama, dragon gods, and the Phoenix.

How ancestors also experience hell

If a spirit eats something that is on the table, traces of the spirit are left in the food. Then when a living person eats that food, the spirit will go in to the person's body and will be trapped there until the person dies. Also, when the person dies the soul of that spirit will become extinct. I asked the gods about this, and they said that when human beings were created, so was this system.

In the evening of July 19th, I finally had some time so I called my father who had not returned in 2 months, and my mother who recently stopped showing up for meals.

My mother said that she was at my sister's house in Fukui, but now could no longer come back. My father said that he became trapped in somebody's body and could not come out.

I knew my father well, so I could image him having something to eat from anybody's dining table without thinking. That was his personality when he was living, and he would eat even when told not to, and I knew he would go to hell. I had become busy with world affairs and the heavy rain in Kyushu, so I thought that it would be fine for him to experience hell for himself. There are also many people who are living that need experience in order to change.

After looking in to it, I found out that my father had entered my sister's body. I asked him about it.

Answer

"It's dark and I look around for an exit with the wish to get out, but I can't at all."

"There were bacteria, viruses, and spirits."

"It was hell. I never want to be there again."

My father had gone to war 3 times, but he said that this experience was the worst hell. I helped my father out of his hell and also helped my mother who had become lost. Then I remembered that 4 ancestors of the Nomura family (father-in-law, mother-in-law, brother-in-law, sister-in-law) had not been back for 4 months.

There was female member of the family who was great grandchild and grandchild in the hospital for cancer, so I knew that they had gone to see her. I had been thinking about it, but now I decided to call my brother-in-law to explain to me what's going on.

Question

"What have you been doing?"

Answer

"Mom and Dad had eaten from a dining table and disappeared, so I couldn't come back."

"I came here to ask for help, but you didn't notice."

"My wife and I are fine."

"If you could call the other 3 now, that would be great."

I called them immediately, and explained to them the process where spirits can become trapped inside of people and animals. I then asked them about their experience.

Answer

"We knew about it, but didn't know that it was such a hell." (mother-in-law and father-in-law)

"It was a place that was so bad it is beyond one's imagination, and I had never experienced such a thing." (father-in-law)

"I don't think any living person has been in such a hell. I don't ever want to be in a miserable place like that." (mother-in-law)

I gave the 3 a meal since they hadn't eaten in a long time. My brother-in-law, sister-in-law, and father-in-law had pudding, and my mother-in-law ate pineapple. I asked how they felt.

Answer

"I feel like I am in heaven just from coming out of the body." (mother-in-law)

"After coming here and talking, I've begun to feel better." (father-in-law)

Question

"Why have my brother-in-law and his wife not eaten?"

Answer

"I wanted to eat, but you didn't ask us to go ahead, so I couldn't." (brother-in-law)

"I wanted to go back to Okazaki as soon as I could." (sister-in-law)

Out of the 4 of them, only my brother-in-law could teleport himself, so the others must be near him in order to go anywhere. That's why my brother-in-law was waiting for his parents. He cares for his parents even after his death. I asked about the grandchild, and apparently she had become better and was living normally.

From knowing about this episode with my family, I think you can understand that spirits can easily become trapped in to the bloodstream of people and animals, and that for a spirit there is no greater hell than this. The best way to prevent this is to tell it to others that you have relations with, so that the same mistake does not happen again. The gods say this also.

A true "kamikakushi," or spiritual disappearance

There was a session on July 26th for the School of Waves, and I received a box of health products from a member that I had been wanting to try.

I looked for bacteria, viruses, and spirits, but it seemed fine, so I tried a pack of it on that day and went to sleep. The next day, for some reason I couldn't find the rest of it, though I looked for it for half a day. I couldn't find it, so I asked about it to my ancestors and to gods in the evening.

"I would like to ask everyone about the box of health products I have been looking for since the morning. I can't find it. If anybody knows about it, can you please tell me?"

The ancestors said they did not know, but 116 gods said they did. I asked for an explanation, and they said that they made it invisible to me because it actually progresses ageing. I was so happy that the gods would take care towards me in this way.

The very next day, there was an email from early in the morning. It was from the woman who had given me the health product. She said she had a fever and some pain from yesterday, and wanted me to look at her picture. I looked at her picture, and the code number for pain came out as negative. She had a kidney stone and gallstone problem, but that wasn't the cause.

On this day I found the box that I had been looking so hard for before. I made a measurement of it, and it came out as the same as her symptoms: inflammation (fever), pain, toxins, and ageing. Also, the places on her body that she was pointing at where she said there was pain came out the same. She had been taking the product mixed with yogurt for 4 consecutive days about 2 weeks earlier, and it affected her after 2 weeks.

If the gods had not let me know, I would not have known that this health product was the cause. Because I was unable to find the box, I was able to avoid drinking it, which saved me from making the same mistake. This time the gods came to the rescue, but most people in the world have no idea about this reality.

There was something else. During these 5 days, I was going through a cold. I would sneeze, my nose was running, my throat hurt, and I was unable to sleep at night. The next day I had to fulfill my duty for volleyball and also do a session for the School of Waves. I wasn't able to even speak, so I became serious and made a measurement for myself, and found out the cause.

A candy that I had had which included honey and ginger

came out as negative for the cold and rhinitis. I think I had about 4 or 5, but among the 16 that were left, the negativity was inside 3 of them. Later, I purified my cold at 4 locations: 2 in the mouth, tongue, and head. I felt much better, and could sleep well. The next day I purified the cold again from my left hand and head, and thought that the cold was completely gone. However, to my surprise, on the 5th day my nose began running again. I got rid of it from my head and felt better immediately. There are many cases where there are still remains of what you purify.

How she experienced pain every day

The session for the School of Waves came on July 26th. The woman who had stayed till the end suddenly began saying "It hurts! It hurts!" while holding the back of her head, so I took a picture.

What I saw were many white orbs. The measurement showed that they were 2 female cosmic spirits with pain and nausea. As I purified her, the pain and nausea gradually decreased, and the woman said that she will do the rest of the purification at her house, and went home.

There were 2 cosmic spirits, and the pain belonged to the daughter, and the nausea to the mother. They had been in the woman's body for 20 years already. They had come from the planet Pleiades to cure their illness, but they became trapped in a dark hell with no exit. I purified them as I talked to them, and the reaction seemed to stop, and they said that their symptoms had gone away.

I reported to the woman about this the next day, but she had begun having a different pain. She sent me a photo of the part where it hurt, and I saw that there was pain from liver cancer belonging to bacteria.

I had a conversation with the bacterium, and the bacterium said it had a child. Before the bacterium fell in to hell, it was in a vegetable field with its child. The bacterium was completely relieved from its pain, and said it will go to the vegetable field to see its child. I said that I hope they will be able to meet, and we parted ways.

I again reported to the woman, and this time she said that her stomach hurt. I couldn't believe that there was another problem, but I couldn't leave her be, so I had her send me a picture to look at. This time it was a virus with kidney stones. Apparently this pain had been going on for a while, with blood coming out with urine. She was in so much pain that she needed pain medication, but the hospital diagnosed her with a bladder infection. I talked to this virus.

Question

"You were human before you became a virus. Do you have any idea why you became a virus?"

Answer

"I was as stubborn as a rock, and did not listen to anyone."

The virus's pain was gone, and it seemed to understand its errors it committed back when it was human. It was reflecting its past in a good way, so I thought that if it makes amends in the spiritual world, it might be able to become human again in its next life.

I again made a report to the woman. But now her back hurt. I was frustrated at the repetition since I was busy, but I looked at the picture she sent me, and saw that there was pain and throbbing in the heart along with pancreatic cancer.

"No wonder you have pain since it's cancer. It's amazing that you have had all these cancers in your organs," I said.

"For some reason when I was a child my heart would hurt, and I would just be bearing the throb, but after that I wouldn't have the pain so frequently, so I didn't make any thought of it," she replied.

The 2 cosmic spirits with heart and pancreas problems were in her body for more than 40 years, and could not even remember which planet they had come from. They were suffering every day, and wished very much to exit the body. When I reported this to the woman, I was quite afraid that she would have more problems, but thankfully the sequence of pain had come to a close.

Asking help from a dragon god regarding the huge Typhoon 5

When I became busy with the woman who was having the various pains, I had become worried about something. A huge typhoon was approaching.

On August 1st I inquired the gods about the typhoon, and they said to seek help from the anacondas. I called the 3 anacondas who became reunited, along with the 2 who were married. However, the husband of the 2 that were married did not show up. I asked what had happened, and the wife answered that he had disappeared without her knowing why. She said she wanted him to return so she could see him. From the satellite image in the internet, I could verify that he had indeed disappeared about 5 days before.

I used the wave measurement of the husband that I had from before to call him over. What he said was that he had become trapped in someone's body, and could not get out even though he had wanted to. It was a horrible place for him and he said he never wanted to go back. I dealt with it right away so they could be together again.

Afterwards, I asked the 5 anacondas to help with the typhoon so that it will not harm the archipelago. But after 2 and a half days, the typhoon just slowed down and seemed to come in to a deadlock. I worried if the 5 anacondas could handle it and decided to ask the gods.

I was told by the gods to call them over and ask. I looked in the typhoon, and saw the brother from the siblings that I had called over in the past, but no sign of the sister. Could the sister be trapped in hell? I called them all over.

I talked to the brother, and he said that he did not know where his sister went and was worried about her. I brought the sister out of hell, and when I asked all of them about the typhoon, the males said that it is too fierce and they need back-up assistance. I had them eat eggs, then sent them back to the typhoon.

I asked the gods again, and I was told to ask a dragon for help. It was my first time to be in contact with a dragon so I was shy, but the gods told me to go ahead so I did with confidence.

Question

"Just now I called 2 male dragons over. May I ask how you feel?"

Answer

"It feels so good it is like coming out of hell and reaching heaven."

Question

"I called you using pictures that were taken quite a while ago. Where have you been since then?"

Answer

"In someone's body. It was a hell with no exit."

Question

"What is the nature of the relationship between the two of you?"

Answer

"We are brothers."

Question

(upon explaining what had been going on) "Can you manipulate Typhoon 5 so that it will not cause harm?"

Answer

"We will try our best."

The dragons went off to help with the typhoon that the anacondas were working at. However, even if 9 of them (the anacondas, big snakes, and the 2 dragons) worked together, this typhoon was a monstrous one that was being reported on daily. After 5 days, I asked the gods again, and this time they said to seek help from dragon gods.

The gods were being careful with the order that things were proceeding.

I was able to call 1 male and 3 female dragon gods.

Question

(upon explaining what had been going on) "This is a fierce

typhoon, but do you have any ways that you could prevent damage on the archipelago?"

Answer

"Yes, if we do our uttermost, then damage can be prevented." (all 4 dragon gods)

Question

"Thank you very much. As of now there are 9 there, of which are dragons, big snakes, and anacondas. What about them?"

Answer

"We will have them help." (all 4 dragon gods)

So off the dragon gods went to help the others. However, after 6 more days, my worries were not gone. Were they fine inside the violent wind and rain without anything to eat? I inquired the gods again, and they said things are going well.

But it had been 7 days and I was worried. I inquired the gods, and they said that the dragon gods have a plan. That's right, I thought. I had asked the experts do deal with the situation, and that was the best idea. The gods had set me straight, and I knew that from then on I should not interfere with their work.

That evening, I thought about the one big snake that I had not called. The female snake who had died from humans burning dead grass and went in to the typhoon to distract herself from the throbbing burns. I hadn't seen her recently in satellite images. Perhaps she was in hell? I called her, and she was indeed trapped.

Question

(upon explanation) "For how long can one go on without sleep or rest when becoming a spirit?"

Answer

"For about a week."

A living person would not last for 2 days, but I felt at ease when she told me this. Then she said that she will go join the others and do her best, and off she went in the rain towards the typhoon. Everybody has been mistreated by humans, yet they go the extra mile without sleep or rest, which makes me respect them very much. I felt the humans who could do nothing were the miserable ones.

Later, on the 8th I looked at the weather satellite, and saw that at 8 pm they were at the typhoon, and that by 10 pm they had all gone back to where they each live. The next day I called them all over to thank them.

Question

"The fierce Typhoon 5 has been stopped by all of you, and the damages have been reduced to a minimum. It is because of your efforts, and I cannot thank you enough for it. By the way, I had heard that a god goes through reincarnation more than 20 times before becoming a god. Is this true for a dragon god?"

Answer

"Yes it is." (all 4 dragon gods)

Question

"Is it a process of a snake becoming a dragon, then a dragon god?"

Answer

"Yes."

Question

"It seems that the number of these souls has gone down."

Answer

"That's absolutely correct. The number has gone down." (all 4 dragon gods)

Question

"The 5 anacondas have been in the typhoon since August 1st, but how do you feel?"

Answer

"It was good to be able to put our hearts in to it with the others." (the 5 anacondas)

Question

"In the case of a mountain fire, could you bring rainclouds over it?"

Answer

"Yes we can." (ten animals and 4 gods)

Question

"When I looked at the world map I noticed 7 other dragon gods, but did you know that they exist?"

Answer

"We didn't really know." (the 4 dragon gods)

Question

"Would you like to meet them if you could?"

Answer

"Yes, we would." (the 4 dragon gods)

Question

"I will call them over when there is opportunity to do so. Would that be all right?"

Answer

"Yes, that would be fine." (the 4 dragon gods)

Question

"Would the others like to meet them as well?"

Answer

"Yes, we would." (ten animals)

I thanked again at the end, and asked for their cooperation in the future. It was a marvelous time indeed. As you can see in the conversation, I was only able to find 10 big snakes, anacondas, and dragons from around the world. Recently when I became friends with them, 5 of them ended up falling in to hell, so the number was reduced to half. Regarding these 10, I can help them whenever, but there is severe risk of losing some of them in this way.

Revelations from God

On July 29th, I lost something important.

I thought that perhaps there was some meaning to this, like the time when I couldn't find the health product. I inquired the gods. They said there indeed was meaning. I asked for a word using Japanese letters, and the word was in 5 letters, spelling "Konutanume." I had no idea what this meant, so I asked if it was correct.

Answer

"It is correct." (75 gods)

"You must understand what these 5 letters mean." (82 gods)

"There is meaning in each letter." (82 gods)

These answers were given by 239 gods including Amaterasuoomikami-sama. An ordinary person like me could not understand what "Konutanume" was. The next day on July 30th I decided to ask again about its meaning.

I asked again with Japanese letters, and this time the answer was 5 words: "Komiwarete," "Nuramimeyuro," "Tarisusochiwatanayoru," "Numumiyami," and "Memuraromuri." They were 5 letters, 7

め	ぬ	た	ぬ	こ
10 め direction... thought/ bud	39 ぬ penetrate	26 た divide	39 ぬ penetrate	16 ⑨ こ roll in/ roll out
13 ① む spread	13 ⑥ む spread	8 り leave	|	3 ③ み reality
31 ら place	3 ⑧ み reality	21 す proceed one way	31 ③ ら place	7 わ harmonize
34 ろ space	15 ⑧ や saturate	30 そ come off	3 み reality	24 れ disappear
13 ⑥ む spread	3 ③ み reality	27 ち condensa-tion	10 め direction... thought... bud	9 て send out... radiation
8 り leave		7 わ harmonize	37 ゆ gush up	
		26 た divide		
		14 ⑦ な nucleus	34 ろ space	
		4 ④ よ new...yang		
		12 る stop		

letters, 10 letters, 5 letters, and 6 letters, making a total of 33 letters which were, according to the gods, from an Ancient language relate to Japanese. I still did not understand. I looked up the website of a researcher of katakamuna letters where there was something called the "Thoughts of the 48 Katakamuna Sounds." I looked at the meaning of each letter, and I was told that the entire meaning's summary would be "Go with your thinking that you have, and proceed within the growth of your thinking ground as you observe reality."

It became August 1st, and when I confirmed this with the gods, they said it was correct. (233 gods) It occurred to me that there could be much more meaning behind these words, so I asked.

Question

"What was the meaning of the word 'Konutanume?'"

1. Message
2. Signpost for the future (guidance)
3. Revelation from God
4. Other

I received the answer that number 3, "Revelation from God," was correct.

Question

"At the end of the revelation there are letters "mu-ri." Does that signify that the things I am talking about will spread, and that people of that place or country will understand it and become independent?"

Answer

"That's right." (292 gods)

Thus August 1st became a day to be celebrated, the day where the revelation was translated and the truth became known. This day was the 17th anniversary of when I began studying about waves also, and this makes me have confidence. But I have not studied about gods or words, so I use the words that come to my mind when I ask gods questions. The way I ask the questions often lack expression or vocabulary, but I ask that the readers use their own imagination.

Mercury, Planet Nanronu, Planet Warayamori……conversations with cosmic spirits

When I have conversations with cosmic spirits, I often ask if there are planets more advanced than Earth. I can't say for sure because I haven't asked about all the planets, but among the many cosmic spirits that I talk to, there are only ones from Mercury.

Mercury is the planet in our solar system that is the closest to the sun, and the temperature of its surface rises during the day to 450 degrees. At night the temperature drops to -180 degrees. A year on Earth is 365 days, but on Mercury it is about 88 days. Earth travels around the sun at 29.8 kilometers per second, but Mercury is the fastest, going at the speed of 47.4 kilometers per second. What it is that it seems nearly impossible for people to be able to live on Mercury, but somehow it is more advanced, which was questionable to me. I inquired the gods about it, and an interesting fact was revealed.

Answer

"They have conquered their shortcomings."

"If people from Earth go, there are places to stay available for them."

"They live in craters."

"There are parking lots on top of roofs."

"Plants grow inside the craters."

"There are oceans and sea creatures."

"A type of electrical power is being used that will also appear on Earth in the future."

"There are no wars."

"Earth should find out why there are no wars there, and learn from them."

"The size of people is smaller than people on Earth."

"People have faces, eyes, noses, ears, and limbs."

"Mercurians are nor greedy."

"They believe in God."

"Transportation vehicles are automated, and everything is set so there are no accidents."

"Eating habits differ from that of Earth."

"They eat eggs and dairy products."

"A man and a woman get married, and children are made."

"Buildings are made with material that overcome temperature."

"There are hospitals, but medicine has not reached the root cause of illnesses (the unseen world)."

I asked a Mercurian spirit who had come that day about things that I had been unable to ask the gods.

Answer

"People live in craters where direct sunlight is out of range."

"There are not a lot of roads."

"There are vehicles like mini-UFOs, and there is a system to prevent accidents."

"People use currency for living."

"People live in buildings and houses, and choose according to preference."

The answers were given by the Mercurian alone, but this day there were those from other planets, including 2 from each of Orion, Lira, Vega, and Nibiru, and 3 from Mercury.

I was able to get backup information which supported what the gods had said, which wiped away my doubts. Later, there was a day where there were 20 cosmic spirits which was a lot, and I asked each of them where they were from. I asked using Japanese letters, which took time, but asking directly is the most certain way. Out of the 20 that had come, 17 of them answered that they were from the planet of Nanronu, and talked to me about life there.

Answer

"It isn't more advanced than Earth."

"There is air, water, and vegetation."

"There are rivers with fish, and we eat the fish."

"We eat plants that grow on the planet."

"We are smaller than people on Earth, and we don't look alike."

"We don't wear anything."

"We don't use currency."

"There are no schools or hospitals."

"There are no buildings."

"We don't give offerings to the dead."

Question

"What made you all come to Earth?"

Answer

"Earth looked like paradise." (all 17)

The next day, on August 31st, 15 more cosmic spirits came, and I asked each of them where they were from. Among them, 14 said they were from planet Warayamorori, and when I asked why they had come to Earth, the answer was that Earth was shining beautifully. I asked about life on Warayamorori.

Answer

"We are not more advanced than Earth."

"There is air, water, and vegetation."

"There are no mountains or rivers."

"We do not do agriculture."

"There are oceans."

"There is a fishing industry, and we catch fish."

"There are no telecommunications devices."

"We use electricity."

After 2 days, on September 2nd, 15 more spirits from planet Warayamorori came, so I asked the same questions, pretending that I hadn't asked them before. The same answers came, along with some other information.

Answer

"There are no animals."

"There are hospitals."

"There are no schools."

"Different areas of land are classified, and people have addresses and names."

At the end I prepared a meal for them. Perhaps it was because their planet had a fishing industry, but they all ate fish, then went home. After 2~3 days, this time there were more from a different planet, so I asked the planet's name. The same name was given by 9 out of 10 spirits. The name of the planet strangely began with a velar "n," and the name was Nrayaerareroyue, consisting of 9 Japanese letters.

Answer

"It is less advanced than Earth."

"There is no electricity."

"There are oceans."

"There are no mountains or rivers."

"There are animals."

"People have hands, feet, a head, ears, mouth, and nose."

"People use cracks in large rocks or caves as dwellings."

"We are called anthropoids."

"Earth seemed like paradise, which is why we came."

After the incidents with North Korea and Typhoon 18 had settled, I began having conversations with spirits again, and another 13 from Nrayaerareroyue showed up. I asked questions that I had missed earlier.

Answer

"We have hair all over our bodies."

"A man and woman get married and have children."

"We are monogamous."

"We can understand the existence of God."

Almost all of these cosmic spirits had come out of the bloodstreams of people. I always say the same thing when I encounter such spirits.

"There are currently tens of billions of spirits trying to run away from the bloodstream they are trapped in, screaming "I want out!" like those I encountered before. However, there are too many, and I cannot help each of them. You are a fortunate minority. No matter how much wealth you have, you cannot use it inside a hell with no freedom. Only the light of God can emancipate a spirit in this situation.

I have received the greatest happiness of my life being able to help you from your pain."

Then I write down itemized choices for answers to give.

1. "I'm glad to be able to come out of the dark place."
2. "I'm glad to be free."
3. "I'm glad to listen to you and understand the causes."
4. "I'm glad that I can go home."
5. "I'm glad that my illness can be cured."
6. "I'm glad of all of the above, and cannot choose."

Everybody chose number 6. Experiencing hell made them understand about suffering very well, so they were all honest and good. Humans, compared to them, only ask God for help when they themselves need it, and do not listen. This is sending the world to a bad direction. I hope that at least one in a thousand or one in a hundred would have understanding, and I would like to march forward with them towards a better future under the guidance of God.

All the souls that have come to my house and gone home after conversations feel the same way, and are trying their best. I have also talked with those from Saturn, Orion, the Big Dipper, Sirius, and Arcturus. Most of these planets are not advanced, with no mountains or rivers. Animals exist on many of these planets, and though the inhabitants receive milk from them, they cannot be so cruel as to kill fellow living beings, and said they feel sorry for animals on Earth. I hope that people of Earth will also be able to have this kind of love.

Conversations with angels

When I began studying blood samples at 3600 times magnification, I wondered if I could find blood that had interesting shapes, and in 1 photo I found something interesting indeed.

It seemed like a person pointing horizontally, and the person had something that looked like wings. There was the shape of a heart on the chest, and something that looked like a crown on its forehead. I made a wave measurement, and the person had high waves that were neither male nor female. From the appearance I could judge that it truly was an angel. I had my grandson draw a picture of it and color it in.

Surprisingly, I was able to have a conversation with the angel. Many of them dwelled inside bloodstreams, in flower gardens, and outside on the earth. They did not eat, and instead consumed "energy."

Around this time, there was program featuring dwarves on television, and when I took I took a picture, as I had thought there was a god-like wave that was neither male nor female at the forehead. I took a picture of the broadcasted feed and called it over, and it turned out to be an angel. It said that it was born because it wanted to be human.

The angel may be living as an angel with a face and wings, or it may also be a soul after its death, in the form of a spherical spirit. Rarely, an angel will reincarnate as a human being.

The ones being shown of television were angels who had been reincarnated as humans. I can understand that family members had thought of them as being kind and adorable. Then I saw that Yoshikazu Mera was making a debut as an actor, playing the role of a fairy. I measured Mr. Mera's forehead, and there was someone that was neither male nor female, having god-like waves. His petite feel and kind personality made the role truly angelic, so he must have been chosen as is because he looks like an angel.

Conversations with animal spirits

Having been talking with gods and various spirits made me think that perhaps I could also talk to animal spirits. I first tried talking to my 2 cats that I kept at my house. I read them the note regarding the cat who had died a centenarian, and my 2 cats said they enjoyed listening to me read very much. I couldn't quite believe that they could understand words, but I asked the gods and the cats later and the answer was that they indeed could.

One day I asked the cats if they wanted to take a walk. Musashi said "yes," while Sasuke said "no," and said he'd rather have a conversation. So I said "Really? Well then I will ask some questions, so Musashi you answer too, okay?" I asked various questions like "Were you happy living here?", "Did you eat egrets?", "Do you have any regrets?", and "Did you know that there are bad things inside drinking water?" When asking the 2 of them, they both answered, and when I asked them individually, they individually answered. This was my last question: "If you were to be born again, would you like to 1. be an animal again; 2. become human; or 3. can't decide on my own?"

They chose answer number 3. I became overwhelmed that even a cat would choose such a brave answer.

One of the members of the School of Waves was having a hard time being possessed by a dog, so I asked the dog an explanation for what it was doing. I had the female dog who had numbness and a panic disorder to come out. Apparently, an accident had caused these symptoms. I had her ascend to the heavens just yesterday, but I called her back and asked where she had been. She had been to the house of her former owner, but the owner was not there. She had been taken good care of when she was living.

Next, there was a woman who would panic when she was in

a vehicle and it turned right, so was unable to ride one. She was possessed with a panic-stricken female dog so I called the dog. I had made the spirit ascend to the heavens a year ago, but I was able to call her back so I did and asked her questions. I asked where she had been for a year, and she said she was with other souls, and had gone to the house of the person she was possessing, and was visiting other souls that had been left. She was drinking water outside. The dog would panic when turning right, and said that she acquired this illness from food. I gave the 2 dogs cheese and water and let them outside.

The woman was also possessed by male dog with a kidney stone that was caused by swallowing tobacco, and another male dog with cold paws and a bad bladder. I asked them about themselves when they came out. Both of them had been trapped, and were finally able to come out. The dog with the kidney stone initially had been possessing a cigarette, but entered the body during inhalation. The cigarette was made in China, and the dog had lived in China as well and died from disease.

Next, her grandson came with her and kept asking for treats even after having one already, so I suspected that it was possessed, and the measurement showed that there was a boar.

A male bear, female bear, male boar, and female boar often show up with this grandson. With the mother's permission, I decided to ask the spirits why they were possessing. The grandfather had been a hunter, and had hunted bears and boars, and I had wanted to confirm about this. As I listened to them, I understood that 1. they were in the breast milk, 2. they were originally inside the foreign-made beverage that the mother drank, and 3. they were from the mountains in China and died of disease. They said they were hungry, so I gave them boiled fish and water, then sent them outside.

On another day when the grandson came again, this time there was a bird, which was unusual. I wondered if a bird would understand me, and decided to ask it questions. The bird was killed and turned in to meat by humans, and was angry about it. I was dumbfounded, but said "I'm so sorry, you must have suffered. You must be hungry, here is some food," and gave it rice, water, and some other food. It ate the food and water, and once I confirmed that it really did, I told it that it was a nice day so it should go play outside with others, and let it outside.

I wanted to talk to the bear that was always there, so I used the picture of the bear that I had purified a year before and called it to ask questions. It was a female cub. It had been a year, so I asked where it had been during that time, and it said that it had been wandering alone, unable to see its mother or friends. The mother had been caught in a trap made by people, and was taken away. The cub was still small so she could not find food alone, and died. The cub said that the grandfather of the person she was possessing used this method to hunt bears. The mother must have been killed after being caught! I felt much pity. She said she was hungry, so I gave her potatoes, salmon, rice, and water. She ate the rice and drank the water. And I told her that in the mountains there are trees with fruit, and that there is a lot of water, so she should go to a mountain with many trees. I opened the door, and she left. I felt so bad for her. I at least wanted to have her meet her mother, and that the 2 of them could live together in the mountain.

All of the animals I encounter go through such misery that it brings tears to my eyes. All of their pain came from human selfishness, and they were oppressing the weak with no feeling of love whatsoever.

In the past, there was great order in nature including the mountains. But now because of development imposed by humans, forests are decreasing. The animals have no choice but to come down from the mountains for food. Humans, without knowing their own fault in the matter, capture the animals saying that they destroy their crop, and even kill the animals. I think that if time and money are going to be spent on that, people should instead plant many trees that will allow food for the animals. This must be the best way for animals and humans to coexist. I believe that people have skills, power, and compassion. I keep wishing that people would have the heart to protect innocent animals.

There is more to this story.

When the cub came on February 10th, I felt much pity and wanted her to see her mother. When the grandson came on February 26th, there was a spirit with a heart disease that came out who had entered the bloodstream from breast milk. That one I had a conversation with, but next came a bear. I had a conversation with it, and it turned out to be the mother who had been killed after being caught in the trap set by the grandfather. She said that she was filled with regret because she had left her cub who could not yet catch food, and that this caused her great suffering. I made a measurement of the waves of the mother bear's emotions, and there was hysteria, worry, and anxiety. The cub's came out as lonely. Even after becoming a spirit, their feelings stayed. It was very sad. I had the waves of the cub from the conversation when she had visited before, so I called her using it. Within a minute the cub came. They knew that they were mother and cub, and said "I missed you so much, I'm so happy that I can see you again." I said "I'm so glad that you 2 could meet again, it makes me cry. Now I'll prepare a meal for you, so please eat it and afterwards go to the mountain to live together happily." They said "Thank you, we will." Then the conversation finished with that, and the 2 of them ate their meal, drank water, and when I opened the door, I was able to see the cub sticking to the back of her mother and them going along. I felt very sorry for them, and felt that I was able to make amends in some way by reuniting them.

Later, I was happily reporting this episode to the others around me.

On February 28th, an animal appeared from over my head, and when I talked to it I found out that it was a female boar. I asked where she had come from, and she said she had been possessing the grandson, and was able to come out of the grandson when he came to my house. She was the mother of a boar that had been killed after being caught in the trap set by the grandfather, and had a daughter. I asked further in detail, and she said that when she came out of the grandson's body, she overheard me talking about the bears. The daughter had gone trying to find her who had died of disease, and found her as meat, and when she was being next to her, she was eaten by the grandson's mother as well. When the grandson was drinking breast milk, the mother bear alone became sucked in, and she became parted from her daughter. So the daughter was inside the grandson's mother's body.

"Is that right! You must have suffered! I'm really sorry about it. I'll bring the grandson's mother here tomorrow if I can, so you can meet your child. Today please eat something here and rest yourself," I said. The boar ate, and went over to the place I told it to go. When I took a look in the morning, I saw that 2 gods had been overseeing the boar from the side.

The next day, the grandson's mother came, and the daughter boar was possessing her at the very top. I immediately had her come out, and asked if she was the boar's child. She said that she was. The mother boar confirmed that it was her daughter. I asked if she had been sending her thoughts, since the daughter was at the very top. She answered that it was the working of gods. Those were words of thankfulness that are hard even for people to say.

When I asked the daughter boar if she was able to find food after mother was gone, and she said that she tried her best and food was found. I said "I'm so glad that you were able to see your mother. I hope the 2 of you will go to the mountains after enjoying a meal together here." They thanked me and said they will go back to the mountains. They ate roasted sweet potato, and flew out in to the sky with the daughter sticking behind the mother tightly.

It was June 26th, and a sequel to the story occurred.

When the grandson came on Sunday, I purified him, and a male bear came out. He had the waves of worry and anxiety, so I had a conversation with him the next day, wanting to listen to him about his feelings. According to the bear, he was killed along with his wife. They were turned in to meat, eaten, and his wife was still inside the bloodstream. He entered the grandson when he was having his breast milk, and finally he was out. He said that he had a child, so I talked about the mother bear and cub 4 that I encountered 4 months earlier, and he said that they were his wife and child. I said to the bear that it could go back to its mountain by himself now that he was free, or I could call his wife and child over for him. She asked that they be called over.

I used the file from 4 months before and called them.

Father: "Were they your wife and child?" "Yes, we finally could meet. I am very happy." Mother and child: "Was this the father? We didn't think we would see him again. We are so happy now." The bears were not visible to me, but I asked "Are you filled with tears of happiness?" The three of them answered, "This is the happiest time ever. We are filled with tears. Thank you."

According to the mother bear and child, since our encounter 4 months ago they had gone back to the mountain they used to live in. Now the father could join them. After they ate the sweet potatoes that I prepared for them, they went off in to the sky.

The New Year of 2017 for my ancestors

Though my husband is not the eldest and therefore not the heir, I have a Buddhist altar in my house with the mortuary tablet for the ancestors of the Nomura family, the mortuary tablet for my mother and father, and also one for my husband. I still don't have a mortuary tablet for my brother and his wife, but they were called by our mother and father and are with them here. I had one for my child who died at age 1, but it was old so we made a bonfire with it and had him join the ancestors. He is now reincarnated as my grandchild, but when he was with the ancestors, he was at the top of the altar.

Later, when my parents and brother had passed away, I purified the souls of my mother and father, and apparently for some reason he became able to move freely, and he had come to the house before anyone knew it. He is in the place he likes in the house, and eats in the living room.

In the morning on New Year's eve, I had the ancestors of the Nomura family take a walk, as usual. It is a daily routine for them to return inside afterwards, but that day they were not back even at dinner time. My husband in the living room was also gone. The others were his parents and brother when he was living, so I thought that they must have all gone back to their old house. Last year everyone was here, but the year before they had also been gone somewhere. That time, my husband had stayed and was eating soup by himself. And before I knew it, the others had returned to the altar. With those previous occurrences, this 3rd year they had all gone back to their old house.

It had become the 6th and they still had not returned. I wondered what had happened. Perhaps there was a reason why they could not get back. I decided to just call my husband back and ask about what happened. I had him teleport his way over, and it didn't even take a minute.

I immediately began asking some questions. First I asked if he had gone to Fukui with them, and also asked how the others were doing. What I found out was that our youngest granddaughter who had gotten married was not feeling well and staying at home. Everyone was worried about her so could not come back. If there is something they are worried about, I wouldn't want to bother them by calling them over, so I decided to let things be for a while. There was no one at the altar from that evening, so I didn't have to prepare any meals. There is always too much to prepare, so I was thinking of having them gather to one place from now on.

Later, I asked the ancestors, and they said gathering to one place would be fine, so I have everybody come eat in the living room.

Then, after having my husband go back to Okazaki by himself, it had been a week, so I asked the 4 ancestors what I should do, and they said to call him back. I called him, and asked if anyone had been troubled, and everyone said that there was nothing else that could be done, so everything was fine. The New Year's disturbance came to a close.

Then in the middle of March, the 4 Nomuras and my husband disappeared again. After about 10 days I called my husband back and asked why. His brother had invited them over to the old house. The granddaughter who was not well before was now in the hospital again. My husband said that because he can perform teleportation, he can go there whenever he wants, so he should probably watch her over from a distance. I agreed. He had been at the place where he had lived and took care of his children and grandchildren. After his death he had become a soul, and had come to Okazaki which he had no relation to, and when he took walks here there were only strangers to be seen around. Even if he could have meals every day, after the meal he could only spend time in loneliness. He wanted to be near the person he loved even though he worried. This must be because he had lived with this person. Ancestors from other families also usually talk about their concerns they have towards their descendants.

A story about a person becoming a bacterium

A certain person was troubled about the sexual center of her husband. That day she brought a picture of her husband asked for a measurement. I soon saw bacteria with a negative sexual center at the top of his forehead. I treated the problem with salt, wanting to having a conversation with the bacterium.

Previously there had been a spirit whose genitals were hurting, who had a negative sexual center and was going through pain there because it had committed rape in the past. News reports of this kind of crime are often given on television. When I see such a news report, almost always I notice the person being possessed by a spirit with a negative sexual center. I decided to ask what had been going on.

I began having conversations with other spirits, bacteria, and viruses included. First, I said "Being able to come out of the bodies they were in and be free was the greatest gift for you! There are tens of billions of spirits around the world are suffering the hell that you had just now been in. They cannot come out, and are struggling. You are fortunate and have been chosen. This was possible due to the light of God, and cannot be done anywhere in the world. I have been given this ability by God, so I have freed you and can also relieve you of your suffering. I can also talk to you. On this paper I have written choices for you to answer from: 1. I feel much better; 2. It is as if I ascended to heaven from hell; 3. I'm still suffering. Please go on top of the answer that is true for you." Then, 3 cosmic spirits and viruses said that they were still suffering. There was still no answer from some bacteria and one cosmic spirit, so I said "There are some of you who still haven't come, but I cannot heal you unless you do, and I should tell you that if you feel fine now I can make you feel even better." I also added "I would like to give a second chance to those who did not come before, so please do." Then 2 who did not reply before came. I raised the quality of all of their waves, and began the conversations, especially with the bacterium.

Question

"Your sexual center is negative. Are you unable to refrain from sexual activity?"

Answer

"That's true."

Question

"What were you before being a bacterium?"

Answer

"A human being."

Question

"What happened when you were human?"

Answer

"I sexually assaulted a woman."

Question

"What was your nation when you were human?"

Answer

"A planet in the universe."

I kept on asking, and I found out that it was a cosmic spirit who had sexually assaulted a woman during life, and when it entered the afterworld with no perception, it had been turned in to a bacterium. Even then, its illness in its sexual center was not better, and its true nature came out. "The man you were possessing did not want to come here. Was this because you were rejecting coming here, that the light of God was too much to bear for you?" I asked. To this, it answered honestly, "I was scared so I was rejecting." We talked as I was purifying everyone, and at the end I said "Do you all feel better now? Wasn't it good that you could listen to the bacterium's story so that you can understand that the things you do affect what happens to you for hundreds of years after death? You should consider it your mission to spread the word to everyone. Good luck!" They gave me a sign saying that they understood. I prepared a meal, told everyone to eat together, and 5 minutes later I asked if they had eaten, but the bacterium hadn't. I encouraged the bacterium to also eat, and it ate crab, which the cosmic spirit also had eaten. Many bacteria and viruses tend to hold back and not eat anything, but once I encourage them to do so, they will eat. They really tend to refrain themselves. I also often send many spirits off from my house every day, and when I say "Everyone, please remember to keep your promises, and good luck," they all line up, then leave together after I open the door. I take a picture saying "Good luck everyone!" How nice they always are! I say to myself. I confirm with the picture I took that they indeed had gone, and can't help but say to myself how nice they are.

Chapter 4

The Afterlife

My child who was born after 42 years!

My son, at age 1 year and 1 month, journeyed off the heaven.

I wrote about this in another book I published before, but now it has been 42 years since my son's death. The past 42 years I have been striving to attain discoveries and a sense of certainty, with the animal spirit being the pathway for understanding the cause of my son's illness along with the help of the picture where the spirit was trying to enter my son from his feet. My efforts have now bared fruit, and I can show the world all the amazing facts that are here in this book. What I'm about to write about contains a wondrous truth that will be told for the first time.

My second son, who was born 2 years after my eldest son's death, had gone through a lot of suffering himself, but married a woman who had relations within the family. Things have gone well between them, and I made measurements for her many times. She is a believer of waves, and I recommended her strongly to my son.

She said that she would like to live separately, so that's what happened, but I had some concerns. Previously during a measurement I found out that there was something possessing her with cerebral infarction and problems with the uterus. Knowing this, I was naturally worried if they could perform the purification by themselves, and of course she was not feeling well, and when things got desperate they called me for help.

Each time, I found out the cause of the problem and got rid of it, but during pregnancy she went to have her blood examined at 3600 times magnification, though she went where there were others in their 50s and 60s, her blood was more jagged and distorted than theirs. The condition was not good. When I measured this blood, there was an overflow of all the things she was going through.

Then one day, she said that she couldn't eat, and there was a cosmic spirit whose stomach was in bad shape. I hurried and got rid of it, and within 5 minutes she said that she could eat again. It doesn't take much time to get better.

She believed in my waves, so she had been bringing pictures of herself when she wasn't feeling well, and sometimes echo photos of her fetus. I was using the Card of Hikari that I had at the time for purification.

Until then, I only saw that there was a soul of a male fetus. However, one day when I was closely examining it, I saw that he had the waves of my son who died at age 1 year and 1 month! I couldn't believe it, but I measured over and over and the results were always a soul of a boy with measles, pneumonia, and a rabbit.

The rabbit with measles and pneumonia had entered my son from his right foot, and water had built up in his right lung. His right lung had to be cut open without anesthesia so that a tube could be inserted to leak out the water. This horrendous procedure was done to him, but he drowned to death anyway. I remember that when his life ended, his head suddenly dropped while he was looking at me during his last moments of suffocation. I wonder if he had wanted to say "Mom, I've done what I was born to do, so now I leave everything to you!" I will never forget his eyes when he was looking at me then.

Ever since I became able to make measurements of the existence of spirits, when I would look at the mortuary tablet in the Buddhist altar, I could see my eldest son at the top of his ancestors. But in August 2014, my eldest son wasn't there anymore. I wondered where he had went, but it turned out in November of that year that he was in the fetus that my daughter in law was pregnant with. But this still made me wonder what he had been doing between August and November. I had an idea about what he might have been doing.

I was measuring my second son and his wife, and when I said that there was a male guardian spirit protecting my second son, his wife said that she wished she also had a guardian spirit. Then my second son said "okay," and gave his hand to her, which resulted in the guardian spirit switching to her instead. I was quite amused by this at the time.

I remembered this small episode and asked them to show

me pictures of them during that time. I measured it, and discovered that my eldest son had been with them both. On August 16th, when my daughter in law entered my house he was with her, and 3 hours later on the same day, my second son had gone a far distance on a mountain hike, and he was in the picture that my second son took at the top of the mountain. He had left the mortuary tablet, then became a guardian spirit for my second son and his wife, then became their child in November.

Later, my husband who had passed away was at the mortuary tablet, so when I had a conversation with him I asked if he had encouraged Naoyoshi (eldest son), to which he replied that Naoyoshi had acted with his own will.

August 1st was the anniversary of Naoyoshi's passing, and I thought that he would perhaps be born on the same day, but he was in breech position so there had to be a Caesarian section. July 30th, the day of the surgery, became his birthday. He looked just like my eldest son who passed away before, and even had the same unique laugh.

Around the 3rd month of his life, he began to cry so hard that his body would almost flip around. With each occurrence I would find out the cause, and the result would be pain from a bone fracture, uterine cancer, and ear tube. Even an adult cannot stand a bone fracture, cancer, or an ear ache. With all of this pain in the fragile parts of his body, he cried hard with a reddened face, and would not stop at all until the purification would help. I felt so bad for him and it just felt absolutely terrible to me. The situation proceeded for days. At the time, I would have to take a picture of the exact location where there was a problem to purify it, so it took time. We wanted to take a picture with his eyes open, but he would shut them when he cried, and my daughter in law said it would take 2 whole hours for the purification. I became motivated to enhance the Card of Hikari in order to save my grandson.

The problem persisted for about 4 months, but thankfully the pains began to fade. The outbursts would occur still, but the situation as a whole became much better.

The pains and things that came out later were partially due to the genes that my daughter in law had, and partially due to the milk. I also studied the breast milk once, and found many causes within it. Breast feeding was done after using the Card of Hikari, but the Card was not able to purify completely at that time. She, as a mother, preferred to breast feed her baby since that was what everybody did, and we would get in arguments because I was against it. My opinion would have differed in the past, but now I am able to see inside the breast milk, so I'd like people to stop, but most people cannot understand.

My daughter in law and my grandson both stepped further in to a state of hell. Later on they finally did what I said. I have nothing but admiration for the strength of my grandson because he had suffered when he had died before, and now he had gone through suffering beyond that of death. He had been fated for a cruel trial.

The Kannon-sama was with my eldest son. And when he became my grandson, the Kannon-sama was with him inside the womb. But it doesn't mean that one's life is easy because a god is watching over. They are fulfilling their purpose. My grandson had a strong spirit to be willingly being born in to such a difficult path. I feel that we must work hard for it to be rewarded.

When my grandson became 1 year and 1 month old, I was told that he had a fever and was not doing well. When I took a look I saw the same symptoms as my eldest son had when he died: pneumonia, measles, and a rabbit spirit. Not only was he 1 year and 1 month old again, but he had the same illnesses, pneumonia and measles, with the same rabbit. It was a mysterious occasion, but though 42 years ago he died from this, this time we were able to save his life.

I had regretted for 42 years that I could not save my eldest son, and it was my dream to at least ease the suffering of my eldest son after his death. With the method that became established over the years, I was finally able to save him. I had nothing but thankfulness. If he had been hospitalized he might have died again. His illness was caused by a spirit in possession of him. Modern medicine denies the existence of spirits, and as long as this is the case, it will fail without understanding the truth.

Now, many animal spirits who were too strong to be purified are coming out. A male bear, a female bear, a male boar, and a female boar. These types of animals have been eaten after being hunted by my grandson's grandfather who was a hunter. My daughter in law had been eating the animals also, so perhaps my grandson genetically inherited some of his troubles. Dogs and pigs have also been coming out, so I have to purify him intently. Even with the 1 bear of my second son, it had ruined his life when he was a child, and when I see examples of other people, there is also much suffering with just 1 animal, which means there are too many animals affecting my grandchild, so I must take great care to purify him.

When I read about this to a god and the god listened, I felt something great in my chest, and tears were flowing out of my eyes. I had to blow my nose many times before finally finishing reading. It was a sad memory for me, but somehow I didn't feel like myself when I was shedding tears, so I asked "Was there anyone helping me shed my tears?" Then 2 gods who were both Kannon-sama said "Yes." The gods who were with me had been walking my path with me from the beginning to the end. They knew everything, so they couldn't help but crying themselves. They've come to experience happiness and grief together with me, and I was grateful towards having this tie with them.

Studies of the soul upon the death of my beloved cat Musashi

On December 29th 2015 my beloved cat Musashi died. His tail was fluffy like that of a squirrel, and his face looked gentle like a little girl, and I always said to him "Why, aren't you the cutest thing!"

Musashi stopped eating his food around December 5th. When I measured him I found pain due to a Herpes virus. I omitted it, thinking it was the cause, but he still had no appetite. Two days later I went out the east side of the house and found feathers of a large bird scattered. I began to worry that Musashi had eaten the bird. Musashi was born from a stray mother cat, and he had been outdoors since being a kitten, eating birds and rats that he caught. At first he would apparently drag his prey in to a room that nobody was in to eat it. I would scold him when seeing the feathers scattered, so he learned to find other places where he could hide while eating. We had given up, thinking that the cat could do nothing about its instincts.

When I took a picture and measured the feathers that were scattered, I found the Herpes virus. It was the same virus that

Musashi had. I remembered that there was an egret in the field that Musashi would go visit. It had large white wings, and now I could not see it. It made sense to me, so I concluded that Musashi ate it, and that he began feeling ill afterwards. I could not notice the beaks or the long legs of the egret where the feathers were scattered, so I realized that Musashi must have eaten all of the egret. No wonder he was sick.

Later we took him to the animal hospital and did an X-ray, but there was no sign of the egret's leg or anything that I thought would be clogged inside. His vomiting was extreme, and he had ascites. His condition was getting worse and worse. It became the end of the year, and he still wasn't able to eat. The 29th was the final day of the animal hospital, and they had done everything they could. We thought that the cat did not have a chance to get better, so I went to the hospital with my granddaughter who was in junior high school and we asked for him to be put to sleep.

Musashi, who now had come home in a box, had liked sashimi so we placed some near us along with some water. After a couple of hours we could hear him making a noise from where he was. My granddaughter got up saying "He said something!" and we looked at each other. Where could he have been making the noise?

"I'll take a picture to see where he is," I said, and when I took the picture I saw that he was above his box by about 1.6

meters. "His spiritual body rose above the box. It must have hurt when it happened, that's probably what the noise was," my granddaughter and I agreed.

I thought I would purify him outside the next morning, but I realized it would be awful to leave him for the night since his measurement had shown negativity with nausea. I purified him in the living room that evening. The negativity such as the nausea turned positive. Along with that, the thing he had eaten became positive, too. This meant that his nausea was gone. As proof, he was eating the things he was unable to when the measurement was negative, and when I place a dish for him he would always eat it. Then I decided to perform an experiment.

Musashi liked sashimi, so he came to the kitchen because he could smell it.

When I told him to "sit," like back when he was alive, he sat behind Sasuke the other cat. He would honor Sasuke, who belonged to this house before he did, in this way when he was alive. I gave Musashi sashimi, saying "Mu, you can eat this too." I put the sashimi in another bowl and put it nearby. He ate. I knew he was there because I took a picture of where the sashimi was and there were waves of a male nauseated cat.

Another time, I was playing with a foxtail, and Musashi came running to it like he would when he was alive.

Also, I saw Musashi lazing in the sun on the futon that I had always been laying out for him so that he could do that.

When he was alive, in the evening I would let him in the house before going to sleep. It has been a year since his death, but I still let him out in the morning to go take a walk and let him in the evening before sleep. I give him food and water every day, and he eats what I give. If even a day went by without noticing him or feeding him, I would worry and probably go out to find him. Late in the evening when I go get him, he usually is waiting at the genkan, so I say "Sorry for keeping you waiting, Mu! Aren't you the cutest!" He is so loveable to me. Because of Musashi and the experiences I have with him, I know that this world and the spiritual world are the same, that they are mirror images of each other. Musashi is indeed the cutest cat ever.

People who have become possessed by foxes

On March 13th 2016, we had a session for the School of Waves which we have been continuing for many years.

One of the participants was not feeling well, and asked to be given a measurement to find out the cause. The chest was where the pain was occurring the most, so I took a picture and found that it was because of a spirit. I looked in to it further, and saw that it was an animal spirit. It was a fox. I informed the participant, who said the together with a friend she had gone to a certain shrine, where upon entering the gate she stumbled, fell, and cut the inside of her mouth. She was given 3 stitches. She also mentioned that she was wearing a fashionable new pair of boots to the shrine. I asked how the fox would feel about this, and the adjacent person said that maybe the fox had become jealous. I entered the code for jealousy and it matched.

The fox had had a personality that was negative in terms of nausea, anger, and jealousy. Being possessed by the fox had made her inherit these features. The fox at the chest was able to be removed by placing the Card of Hikari on the camera with the fox for just 3 minutes. The purification was complete and the fox went to heaven, and the nausea at the chest was gone.

When this problem was solved, someone showed up who was quite late, and I said "You're quite late!" To this she replied "I could have come sooner but I was going in circles around the same place. It was as if a fox had grabbed hold of me!" We all laughed, because we had just had an episode with a fox also.

"Weren't you being possessed by a fox, too?" someone said, and we decided to take a picture of her, and indeed she had been possessed by a fox. "See?"

I asked her since when she had been in that situation. She said she hadn't noticed, but the fox came after stopping by at her friend's house before coming here. I told her it was possible that her friend had something to do with it, and asked if she had a picture of her friend. She said she didn't have anything, which was too bad. She said that her friend had problems in the bronchi, and because she herself had been coughing repeatedly, I decided to study the fox in detail. I found out that the fox had bronchial asthma. The fox had possessed her when she was at her friend's house, and not only was she to bewitched on her way, but she had been given problems in her bronchi. I purified the fox with the Card of Hikari and let it go to heaven. The session that day was concluded with laughter and fun regarding the fox incidents.

Daily life of ancestors and conversations with them

After understanding clearly that my beloved cat, though I could not see him, was living in the same dimension as me, the same way he was when he was alive, I started to think that perhaps my ancestors would also like to take walks. Just during that time there were amazing violet lavenders growing behind my house, and they were near the Buddhist altar, so I opened the window and asked my ancestors if they would like to take a walk. Afterwards I took a picture and saw everybody over where the flowers were. I kept the window open, and shut it after confirming that everyone had gone back. After realizing this, I began wanting to allow them to take a walk every day, so

I continued.

I made some observations, and one of them was that my father in law and mother in law were always back early. They are close with each other, and are always together during the walk. Otherwise, my sister in law seemed to be alone, away from the others, but my brother in law seemed to be watching over her from a distance. The Buddhist altar currently is holding 4 members of the Nomura family.

Also, currently in the living room there is my father from my side of the family, along with my mother , and my husband. However, previously my eldest son who had died at age 1 year and 1 month was at the altar and mortuary tablet in the tatami room, along with his ancestors(?) and my husband. My eldest son became the son of my second son and my grandson on July 30th 2015, so he was gone. My husband one day decided to hover over my head, but now he was in the living room, and he eats the meal that I prepare for him every day. And when we were laying my brother's ashes to rest, I purified my mother and father who were in their graves, which made them able to move freely, so now they move freely inside the Nomura residence and have their meals in the living room.

I was making various discoveries in May, and wondered if I could talk to the ancestors. I could measure spiritual wave, so perhaps I could ask questions and get answers in either yes or no.

I immediately began the experiment. On a piece of paper, I wrote the question in the middle and "yes" on the right, "no" on the left. I asked some questions, and all 7 of them answered. What brought you here? Is it comfortable in the Buddhist altar? Are you happy with your meals? Do you get cold or hot? Do you want to be born again? They answered many questions. I also received answers from individuals, such as what disease caused them to die, like stomach cancer or vaginal cancer. They each possess their own wave, so I can tell who it is. The conversation is all recorded photographically, so anybody can confirm it if they can use the wave measurement device.

I would like to give the example that left me with the strongest impression.

Out of the questions that I asked to the Nomura ancestors, I had also asked about the meals I serve them every day, whether they are satisfied with the taste or the quantity. My mother in law and sister in law said "yes," while my father in law and brother in law said "no."

So I asked further for the ones who said "yes" and the ones who said "no" to give me more details about how they feel out of 1. It tastes bad; 2. I would like something that tastes better; 3. There's not enough; 4. I want cigarettes; 5. Other. My father in law and brother in law answered number 5, "other." What could "other" mean? Two days later, my sister in law was eating with the other 3 from the same plate, thought she had previously been eating alone.

After this, I asked the ones who answered "other" again, this with the choices of 1. I want to eat pickles; 2. I want to eat fish from Fukui; 3. I want to drink alcohol; 4. There are 3 offerings being made but 1 is fine; 5. One offering for Buddha and 2 for the rest of us is good; 6. Other. My brother gave the opinion of number 4, that everyone should eat from the same place. I think my brother told my sister that she should eat with everyone, out of thoughtfulness towards me. The brother was the one who held authority during life, and after death he is making decisions about everyone in the same way. Thanks for him I am able to simplify my duties now by giving 1 offering on 1 plate.

I have a spiritually uplifting story from the old house that I grew up in.

I had been listening a lot previously, but recently I was having more conversations with Kanzeon Bosatsu-sama, so I wasn't able to have time. However, though it had been a while, I decided to talk to him.

"Kazuo (my husband), sorry that I haven't been talking to you lately! You're always watching me do my work, so you must know about developments in detail, but did you know that now I've found out a great truth?" To this question, my husband answered, "I'm always beside you, so I know!"

Then, I had my father and mother teleport themselves over

to me from the tatami room and the 2nd floor. I asked them to give answers from the following choices:

1. **Us Mom and Dad, we were both in a different room, but we had the wondrous experience of arriving here.**
2. **Fumiko, we are thankful because ever since coming to your house we have been feeling better and there is food.**
3. **We were in the grave for a long time, but we were not happy because it was dark and there was no food.**
4. **It is heavenly compared to before. Thanks!**
5. **Everything from 1〜4 is correct.**
6. **If something is incorrect, please choose from 1 through 4.**

They all answered number 5, that it was all correct.

I thanked them for their reply, and asked if there was anything else they'd like to say. My father, mother, and husband all said there wasn't anything.

There was something else that I had wanted to ask, but I wanted to ask it in Fukui together with my siblings. However, I did not have much opportunity to go to Fukui, so I went ahead and asked:

When Mom and Dad were alive, when there was pain in the body we were go on the train to take a trip! Where did we go?

1. Takefu; 2. Fukui; 3. Nagahama; 4. Sabae. Everyone answered number 3, Nagahama. I was so deeply moved that I wept, and asked the next question while crying. We always bought souvenirs! We bought 1. Chocolates; 2. Steamed buns; 3. Fruit; 4. Sweet rice jelly(Uiro). Everyone answered number 4, sweet rice jelly. I knew that they were always there, but having these things about the past confirmed made me weep even more, knowing with greater affirmation that their presence was real, and that they remembered when they were alive.

When I was in my old house, family members and neighbors would always go to the clinic in Nagahama whenever they were hurt or felt pain in their limbs or lower back. They would always get sweet rice jelly on the way back as souvenir.

Someone who lived in the 2nd floor of our house

It was May 28th 2016. I had become able to have conversations with spirits, and when I was taking pictures on the 2nd floor I found many white orbs appearing in the photos. I studied them in detail, and found out that there were 4 of them, with 3 males having great problems with their ligament, anemia, Beta waves, along with a female who had an ovarian tumor problem. I asked them a few questions.

- **"How did you get in?" To this they answered "From**

the 1st floor." (everyone)

- The reason we came was that this house seemed like a place where we could be saved. (everyone)
- Our suffering from when we were living is still here. (everyone)
- I'd like to eat, but I'm withholding myself. (ligament, anemia)
- There is nobody who will give me offerings. (ovarian tumor, Beta waves)
- It would be nice to be protected from wind and rain. (ligament anemia)
- It would be better than a grave. (ligament, Beta waves)
- I'd like to sleep on a futon if possible. (ovarian tumor)
- After giving a meal, I found out that it had been decades since the last time she ate. (ovarian tumor)
- It has been so long that I feel like this is the first time since death to eat. (Beta waves)
- I'm happy. (ligament, anemia, Beta waves)
- If we could have food again we would be very happy. (ovarian tumor, ligament, anemia)
- We are sorry for disturbing you and are speechless. If you could just keep us here. (ligament, Beta wave, anemia)

Otherwise, they said things like how they could not enter if there was a screen at the window, or how they'd like to be born again soon, or that they sleep when they are sleepy, and that it was better for them to have something to do.

I would feel sorry for them if I kicked them out, so every other day I take a meal upstairs for them.

The story continues.

It was March 28th 2017. For the past 10 months the 4 of them had stayed in my room upstairs, except for when it was time to eat, where then they came downstairs. However, from this evening, there became no evidence that they had eaten. I remember that the night before when I went to bed, I had said something to myself about the wonderful experiences I've been having with the purifications and conversations. "They are all so nice! Each one of them listens to me, and say that they will do their best. I think they become thankful because of the suffering they've gone through." Perhaps they were moved by what I had said, because the next day they were gone.

The issues of a person who was a detective in a previous life

One day, after becoming able to have conversations with spirits, I took a picture in the tatami room, I found the waves of a person other than my ancestors, which was unusual. Sometimes such a person would have bad waves, and when that would happen I would tell them that they didn't belong there, that there are too many like them that need help, and that their suffering is the result of their actions during life. Then I just purify them and kick them out.

This person's waves weren't negative, so I decided to see what was the cause of death. It was prostate cancer. Someone in my neighborhood who was in the same cemetery had also died of prostate cancer recently, so thinking there was a connection, I decided to ask that person questions.

In the morning of June 16th 2016, I said "I will now inquire to the one who has been here since the other day," and asked some questions. As I had guessed, he was a detective during life, and had done his job well and was mourned for his death by the people in the area that he had lived in. He always had a smile and I had liked him also. Now he was in my house, and he said that he had something he wanted to say.

I thought that it would be better if his wife was also listening, so I went to her house, which was only 5 minutes away by foot, and explained what was going on. Her only reply was that Amida-sama had taken him to heaven 49 days after his death, and that he was no longer here. There was nothing I could do, so I returned home.

On a later date, I asked the detective (he had probably gone to see his wife with me) something. "Your wife is quite a stubborn woman, isn't she? Because I want to save as many as I can,

I try to talk to only those who can understand, but I liked you a lot, so I hope that I can help you as much as possible." I then asked some questions, and received the following answers:

1. What we had believed in. 2. Regarding offerings, Buddhist altar, grave, and meals. 3. Other.

When he came again another time, I asked some other questions. Are you receiving any meals? To this he answered "no." When I spoke with him the other day he had received his offering, and I had even taught about the way to do it. I couldn't believe what I heard, so I asked for an explanation. I thought that he couldn't get inside because everything was locked, or that the offerings weren't given the way they were supposed to, or that there were other possibilities, so I asked everything I could imagine, but the only answer I got was "other." I became very puzzled.

I asked if cosmic spirits had been coming to eat his food, which was quite improbable, but the answer was "yes." Oh my goodness! How could he know? Was it the intuition of a detective? I myself have a hard time measuring cosmic spirits, so I wanted to know how he knew.

"Based on your previous answer, please tell me why you know it is a cosmic spirit." I gave him the following choices: 1. From the smell; 2. They have a different spiritual body from humans; 3. They have no manners; 4. Other. His answer was "other."

What could "other" be? I really wanted to know, so I decided to ask the answer letter by letter using the 50 Japanese letters. There was the answer "rohonuho" which was 4 letters, but I could not comprehend what it meant. I asked if it was really correct, and the answer was "yes." It wasn't in the dictionary, people that I asked said they didn't know what it is, so I wondered if it was some special detective term. Then I looked in the kotowaza (proverb) section of the dictionary, and found it! It meant bride, selfish, troublesome, and naughty. I then asked again, and he answered that there were 3 who were selfish and naughty who were eating from the Buddhist altar. Because of this the detective could not eat, and I don't know if it was because he was a detective, but it seemed that he wanted justice.

On a later day I spoke with his wife, and she said "Please tell him that's he's already worked very hard, and that he must rest in peace!"

When one dies, one becomes a sphere the size of only 3mm, unable to do anything, having no arms or legs.

However, spirits live in the same spiritual world for over 500 years, and there they have emotions, and eat meals.

People are unable to know this truth, and many religions are born, and people all believe in what their religion teaches about after death. Because of this, many spirits feel out of place, that they cannot eat, have pains, and are suffering.

Even I had, till recently, been vaguely thinking along the same line as other people. Because I have become able to have conversations with many beings, now I have begun coming to terms with the truth, by asking about my doubts one by one.

As I was studying the offerings that I was giving to my ancestors, I found out that sometimes the detective was there eating, too. In the morning the next day, I opened the door to let Musashi out for his walk, and the detective had also gone out. I assume that he had gone back to his wife. I feel bad that I wasn't able to help. If I could, I would go to his Buddhist altar, pay respect, and purify the cosmic spirits but I cannot.

Thanks to my 100 year old beloved cat

All of the cats in my house were stray. Sasuke was the only one who could live his life to the end here, since the others had died illness, an accident, or had become lost. He spent 20 years with me, and if you calculate that in to human years, he would be 100 years old.

Sasuke himself, in the long life that he had, once wasn't able to urinate for 4 days because of bladder cancer inside the powder I gave him, and also once could not eat for 4 days because he was possessed by a dog with stomach cancer. He had been through many crises, but this time not only was he old, but the main cause was the things contained in the food he had been eating had caused him to be unable to drink water.

This does not mean that the company that made the cat food intentionally poisoned it, but that unfortunately by accident the food became a product with the contaminant inside it. This is not just a matter of pet food, but also with food that people eat, medication, and health products. The contaminants cause various things, such as cancer or a bad personality. In general, because many people at once will suffer from a norovirus, food poisoning, or the flu, the cause is then said to be from food. Even if 1 individual or 1 household did have that cause, the reality in this world is that the cause can never truly be known.

However, I attained knowledge of the existence of waves that cannot be seen by the naked eye 17 years ago. And by working with it I have learned to be able to discern the root cause of illnesses.

Furthermore, this time with the death of Sasuke, every detail of the process towards going to the other world became practically demonstrated in perfection through 17 years of research, practice, and results.

From around January 15th, he could not eat or even drink water, which he loved. He would come near it but could not drink. He laid in his spot sleeping every day. I thought there was nothing that could be done since he was old, but I hoped that when the time came he would be able to die in peace. But he hadn't had water in 3 days. I wished that he could die peacefully after having some water. I was purifying him, but could not figure out what was wrong. I would enter various code numbers for things such as "kidney," "stomach," "liver," "bronchi," "cancer," and "pain," but still no answer. What was wrong? It was so terrible that he could not even drink water, which he loved! I would try getting him to drink using a syringe, but it would cause him to have an expression of so much distress even with one drop, which he could not drink.

I was thinking by myself, wishing badly to figure out the cause of Sasuke's illness, and remembered the face he made when I gave him 1 drop of water. It occurred to me then that it could be his chin, and I entered the code number for "chin illness" which turned out to be correct. That was it! Negative 10 for chin illness, and negative 10 for nausea. It wasn't a small number by any means. I had been purifying him, but with the number I knew it was too late. After knowing this, I purified everything that had appeared, and he was able to drink water for the first time in 4 days. The chin illness would appear every 2 hours even though I purified it. It was when the number of what had appeared became 0 that he could drink water. However, it had been 10 days since he had eaten, so I became prepared that he will die.

I thought that I should talk to the gods at this time.

1. Keep purifying and watching over Sasuke.

2. Take him to the hospital so that he can either receive an infusion or be put to sleep.

3. Other

I asked which of the 3 above were correct, and the answer from the 4 gods who were all Kanzeon Bosatsu-sama was "other."

I wasn't sure what "other" meant, so I asked again.

They said that I should give him words of thankfulness and appreciation, and speak to him of the memories I have of him spending time with me as family over the years. They said he will have a peaceful death. Now I knew what I should do. Everything was clear.

When he became unable to drink water, I would lay down a futon to sleep next to him at night. About every 2 hours he would be moaning, and bad things would appear at a great quantity. After purifying it in a hurry, he would become at ease and go back to sleep. The same thing would happen during the day, and he would calm down after I purified him. This happened repeatedly, and I began to wish for him to be able to die with no pain than to go through what he was. When he had an attack from his heart disease, I rushed to get rid of the symptoms, and his suffering became elongated, not being able to die. Towards the end, symptoms would arise every 10 minutes (from the illness that he had within his body for a long time), so I kept on purifying him, being surprised by the increasing frequency, and at the very end he was able to go in peace with a thoroughly purified body.

To confirm the identity of a spirit after death, you need some kind of a mark so that you know who it is. Usually it is the illness that they died from, but in Sasuke's case, I had purified him so much that the only measurement I would be able to make with his spirit would be "cat" and "male." In this case I wouldn't be able to tell him apart from other cats, so what I did was when I previously had noticed a measurement with Sasuke that read "coccygeal nerves: negative 20," I decided to leave the problem as it was. It was a rare condition and wasn't that serious of an illness, so I wanted to use it as a way to identify Sasuke.

However, I had been purifying many of Sasuke's problems as soon as they would arise, so I was worried whether the coccygeal nerve condition was still there. I fearfully looked at the forehead of the corpse, and saw that some of that condition was left. With this as a mark, I would be able to identify Sasuke's spirit, and if by any chance he became lost, I would be able to call him back, so now I wasn't worried.

When I knew that Sasuke had his coccygeal nerve mark, I decided to draw out his soul from his body. About a year before when Musashi, my cat, had died, after 2 hours there was a sound made by him as his soul came out of his body. Because of Musashi, I have come to understand a great deal about the aftermath of death over the year, and this understanding made me want to try this experiment. I performed the experiment 45 minutes after Sasuke's death, and it didn't take long for the soul to come out of his body. After an hour, I saw evidence of him drinking water twice that was offered. He must have had it twice because he wasn't able to drink water before. At night, he was eating salmon which he loved with Musashi. Being able to eat is a sign that the body after death is healthy. When one dies from an illness, even if the person's descendants give offerings, the meal cannot be had until healing is done.

Even though Sasuke died, because I know very much about what occurs after death, I did not cry. What I did the first thing next morning was take a picture. Wondering where he had slept, I then began to cry. It was because I saw that Musashi, who had died the year before, was lying next to him asleep. My husband was watching over them from aside. What a world, where everyone is watching over Sasuke during the first night of his death! It was a view that flowed with love and care. I could not help but cry, saying "Thanks, Musashi! Thanks, Dad!"

The story continues. After I wrote this part of the book, I read it to the gods, the ancestors, Sasuke, and Musashi, to get their feedback. I first told them my intention, then read it aloud to them twice.

I asked them to choose from the following:

1. It was very good!

2. Some parts are wrong.

3. There are some extra and unnecessary parts.

4. There's something that should be added.

5. It's all right.

6. Other

The 4 gods who were Kanzeon Bosatsu-sama, my husband, my brother and his wife, Sasuke, and Musashi all chose number 1, that it was very good. I was dubious at first towards getting an answer from Sasuke and Musashi, but the measurements read 2 cats, "coccygeal nerves" (Sasuke) and "nausea" (Musashi). I thought it may have been a coincidence, so I decided to ask everyone again.

I thanked everyone for the response. Sasuke and Musashi also answered. I then asked everyone if they could understand human language. I asked them to choose from:

1. No

2. Yes

3. Other

I made "yes" be the second one on purpose.

However, all the responses were number 2.

I was flabbergasted that animals could understand language. It then occurred to me that actually it had seemed like they knew what I was saying while they were alive. There were certain times when it really seemed like it. If this is true, then how fun the world is!

Ever since beginning to have conversations, anybody who had been staying late would stay the night over and leave the next day. Upon such an occasion, I became sure that God watches over everybody at all times. How were things with Sasuke? I decided to take a look.

I had known that Musashi and my husband had been beside Sasuke, watching him over on the night of his death, but now I knew that 4 gods were also watching him over. The gods gave their love without discrimination. I thank them deeply.

Conversation with a satanic spirit who dwelled inside blood

One day, after purifying a person who was possessed by satanic spirits, I went ahead and had a conversation with those spirits. At the end when I asked how they physically felt, many cosmic spirits and Cells said that they had become very much at ease. However, 2 of them said that there was no change in their condition and that they were still suffering. They were human spirits, and had the measurements of "Satanic," "pain," and "bladder" being negative. They were still in pain regardless of the long time I spent purifying them, so I wondered if they were being punished for their behavior during life. I decided to ask them about it. These answers came as a result:

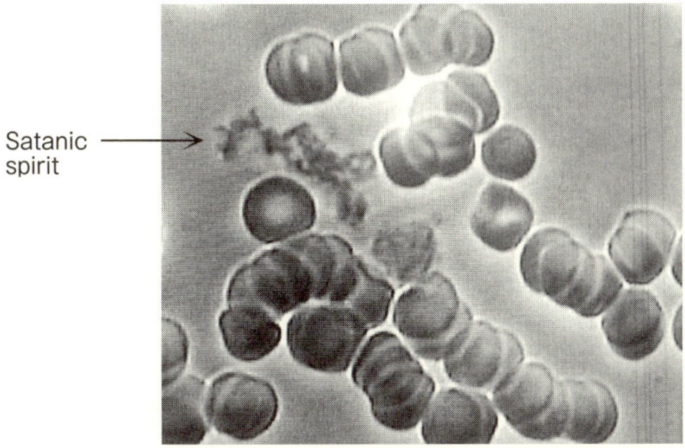

Answer

"The 2 of us conspired to commit a crime together."

"We paid for the crime in prison."

"We committed murder by having the victim be in an accident to receive money from his insurance."

"The pain of the person who died is coming to us."

"Now we are in 2 hells, the crime we committed, and being stuck in someone's bloodstream."

"We are full of regret."

Then, as I listened to them, loose ends became tied together in my mind. There was a Satanic spirit with horns walking inside the picture that I got out for this book. I made a measurement, and they had the same waves. Discovering this could only have been done through the guidance of God for sure.

Chapter 5

Experiences Having to do with Anybody Being Able to Purge

Testimonial of a person who became well from practicing wave purification

Here I have testimonials of people who got better through the practice of wave purification. The first 2 examples and the last one are written by me regarding the experiences of people close to me or about myself. The others have been contributed by members.

ALS myasthenia disease (my niece/resident of Fukui prefecture/64 years old)

In February of 2012, I received a sudden phone call from my niece, who said that she could not sleep due to pain in her knees and shoulders. After having an MRI done, they said that she had a problem with her meniscus, and though she felt better after receiving a knee injection, her hands and shoulders then began to hurt. She slept while leaning on something sitting up in her futon, but couldn't really sleep because of severe pain. Her biggest wish was to be able to sleep.

I told her then that facts about her condition could not be found out anywhere, and that I wouldn't be able to cure her at all unless she came to Okazaki. Her condition must have been bad, since she came straight away.

She had a chronic chilblains problem, and she had terrible chills in her hands and feet. I got rid of it, but the next day another chronic condition of hers came up. It was a febrile disease that made her face become bright red due to a virus, which I also got a great quantity rid of. After that she seemed to be much better, and her worst problem of not being able to sleep due to pain was gone. She could now move her arms out in front of her, but still could not reach behind. I asked her to take a picture and send it to me by email. With that picture, I found out that there were bacteria causing myasthenia gravis, a spirit with a meniscus problem, and a cat bothering her ligaments. The myasthenia gravis bacteria were making her feel heavy like she was carrying a child on her back, and when I got rid of it she smiled, saying "Oh, much lighter!" As I got rid of more of the causes of her problems, she would be able to bend her arm, or the pain would cease. There was much joy as I continued to solve her problems, and she felt even lighter, and became able to stretch and twist her hand which she was unable to do before, now doing so to a great degree. She then happily went back home.

Upon reaching home, other conditions that were within her would begin to appear. She was purifying by herself and became better, able to move, but she was unable to relieve herself from the pain she had in her shoulder. When she would move her hand upwards or behind her back, something would get stuck, and she was unable to stretch further. She was now back here for the 3rd time. There was a sad spirit with myasthenia gravis, and a virus that caused arthritis. It was all concentrated on the shoulder that hurt. The virus caused inflammation so it was swollen, but after getting rid of the virus the swelling was gone and she said that she felt better. It was the 3rd time and the number had become less than half, with no pain the next day, and she was in such good condition that she could exercise while stretching out her arms and legs. She went home, and afterwards was able to do her chores and take walks, but now became worried about her daughter and sister. Looking back, it had been 3 months exactly, and there had been a new kind of spirit, bacteria, or virus each time she came. What I see now is that all of the bad conditions that had been within her reached the limit and there was something like an explosion. If she had had those symptoms in old age, she wouldn't have been able to take care of it all by herself. She wouldn't have been able to come to Okazaki by herself, and of course I wouldn't be able to go see her so many times. I think that she was fortunate that the symptoms would arise while she was still young. I also feel that it was her ability to keep the faith and continue pursuing treatment that brought her the results.

A kidney stone 25 km away disappeared through teleportation (Nagoya City resident/45 years old)

On September 16th 2016 there was a television program revealing the various techniques of people with psychic or supernatural abilities. The viewers could only express words of disbelief and incomprehension. I was watching the program that day, and decided to record it so that I can find out the secrets to the magic. I made measurements of the 20 people who appeared on the show along with some other main aspects. I had thought that magicians like them usually were helped by animal spirits, but this time I saw that more than half of them were accompanied by a Kannon-sama, which surprised me. The Card of Hikari allowed me to inspect the genetics of these people deep within their brows, which helped me realize this. The magicians must have been given the role of showing people that there are phenomena beyond the realm of scientific thought that exist in reality.

That day there were many unthinkable things shown, for example the teleportation of an object over the distance of 80 meters, or something going through an obstacle made of glass.

That day, I was supposed to get a phone call in the evening from a person named T, but I didn't even get a call the next morning, so I called instead. He said that after the call yesterday his lower back started hurting so much that he could not walk unless he bent himself over, and not only that but he had a fever. Unable to call me because of his pain, he wasn't even able to get any sleep. He said that right before it began to hurt, he had been at the hospital getting an ultrasound to check his chronic kidney stone problem that he had had for the past 30 years. The pain had gradually gotten worse after he left the hospital to go home.

I always tell people to bring a copy of the picture if they have had an X-ray or an ultrasound. T said that he had a picture of his fatty liver and the stone, so I told him to send it to me using the internet immediately.

The measurement gave a negative reading for the stone problem, liver, fat, and pain with the greatest amount of bacteria that I had ever seen. I purified the picture outside at once. Everything went from negative to positive, ascending to the heavens. I assumed that this would end T's pain, but when I called him he said that he was better but not completely, so I asked him to send a picture of where it still hurts and his forehead.

What was then sent to me was a picture that showed a greater number of kidney stones, a female spirit that was sad and had a negative measurement for pain, and the same number and symptoms on the back where it hurt and on the forehead. The forehead had even contained data about the lower back. What that means is that by purifying the forehead alone, the lower back can also be purified, which is amazing. You can purify either one.

After purifying the picture of the lower back and seeing that it went up in to the heavens, I called him after 30 minutes, he said that the pain increased dramatically right when I began the purification, and when he felt something pulling the place where it was hurting, the pain began to fade, and it was right when I called him that he was feeling like his old self, which he said joyfully.

What I did was place the Card of Hikari on the picture that was sent to me (the picture can still be in the camera) for 5 to 10 minutes. She does do it herself, but because there was a great many, and that a kidney stone is a special kind of problem, there wasn't enough light that she could give to purify it. I had to put in all I had to be able to purify it. I think that there will be progress from the learning experience that this brought.

Though I lived in Okazaki and she in Nagoya, we were 25 kilometers apart but all I had to do was shine the light of God on the picture and it didn't take a minute for it to reach her and remove the bacteria for the stone, fatty liver, and pain, along with the spirit for the kidney stone, pain, and sadness. It all went up in to the heavens by teleportation. The spirit who had died because of the stone also became relieved of pain and sorrow the same way. Everything becomes happy, and this happens in a matter of minutes. However unbelievable, it is true. The magicians have also shown unbelievable things. Whoever is reading this book must be a fortunate individual who has the ability to believe.

The story continued on the day after. Yesterday T had gotten better, so I called her to see how she was doing. She said that some pain remained from yesterday, and along with that she had a headache, so she was purifying them. I thought that it was strange for her to be having any pain, so I asked her to send me a picture of where it hurts and her forehead. I took a look and saw that it was a kidney stone. I studied carefully and saw that there was a spirit of sorrow, but compared to the female one who had the problem in her 10th thoracic vertebra, this one was a male who had a problem with his 6th thoracic vertebra. It was a different spirit with a kidney stone. I had him ascend to the heavens around 3 o'clock, and she said that her pain diminished around then, along with the headache and odorous ovarian cancer. I looked at the sky and I could see that the purification was a success. They had been dwelling inside T and I had studied them when they came out, so now there is record of the odor belonging to the cancer and the pain being due to the headache. It was a day with new discoveries.

The experience of my 82 year old mother with cholangitis

(Okazaki City resident/61 years old/female)

It has been about 15 years since meeting Nomura sensei and coming to know about waves. I have been surprised over and over by its research. The reasons behind illness, pain, and throbbing. Natural disasters such as earthquakes and typhoons.

Not only those, but even the causes behind crimes such as murder can become obvious. The methods to solve and prevent these things can also be revealed. I was taught many things, and had many of my problems solved. I'd like to talk about a couple of those things. What I'm going to talk about happened to my mother, not to me.

It was about 2 years ago, 6 months after my father had passed away. Things had calmed down. My mother was 82 years old at the time, living by herself. At the end of September I was told that she was taken by ambulance, so I rushed to the hospital. They had saved her life, but she was in no safe condition. The diagnosis was cholangitis (a gallstone becomes unable to exit the bile duct, causing inflammation) and a stress fracture in the lower back. The lower back hurt so much that she could not get up or turn over.

The doctor said "Cholangitis is best treated through surgery, except that in your mother's case, because of her age and obesity problem it would be too dangerous. The only way is to treat it through medication, but that may make her bed-ridden even though she has her fracture. Even if she is able to leave the hospital, I recommend that she moves to a nursing home. She can't go back home, there's no choice."

Any person would have given up. But I knew how she could get better. I decided that I would have to do it myself. I started with her lower back which hurt so badly that she couldn't move. At that time there was no Card of Hikari like there is now, so I placed salt and the necklace. I could go to the hospital only once a week, so I only did it 2 or 3 times, but before a month went by gradually her pain faded, allowing her to sit and walk. Next was the cholangitis. I placed salt and the necklace on her back over and over. I didn't know the exact location in her body so I switched places as I did it. My mother said that when I would place the necklace against her, it would feel like something is flowing out of her like there's a vacuum cleaner and that it was making her feel more comfortable. The inflammation of the cholangitis became better, and in 3 months she was able to leave the hospital. The doctor who said she won't be able to walk exclaimed that her recovery was odd, flabbergasted that she had gotten better. My mother had been staring at her hand, saying "It must be my time now. It's no good," getting herself ready to die. But she had held on because she had to do things for the passing of one year since the death of her father.

Every time I went to the hospital, I would get salt and the necklace and place them against the place where it hurt. The method I was using was quite different from "common sense," but she must have been desperate enough to allow me to do what I wished without knowing the reason behind it. That's how she got better, and she accepted it.

The other experience I had occurred while my mother was

still in the hospital. It was when my mother became able to walk and the bed was moved from the hall side to the window side. By then she had recovered so far that she could take a shower.

I went to see her and said "Oh, you moved over to the window! How nice, since it's brighter then." Then I noticed something odd. There was an odor. The odor was immense, and it came from my mother. It smelled like rotten oil. And then I remembered there being an explanation about cosmic spirits at one of Nomura sensei's meetings. I believe there is a more detailed explanation in a different chapter, but apparently there have been many measurements of souls with no spinal cord, and they are neither human nor animal because they are cosmic spirits. You can tell if they are male or female, or if there's something wrong with them, and this time it appeared with bromine, having a unique smell. They have been appearing in various places over the recent years. I knew how to get rid of this problem because it was taught to me, so I went home without saying anything, planning to be ready on my next visit. The next time I went to the hospital, it was the day that she was leaving, which turned out to be a good thing. I took my sister and mother home, and right when I began talking about the odorous cosmic spirit, my mother said "That's it! Whatever's possessing me, it stinks, and I kept asking the nurse if there was something wrong with me like a disease, and she would just be silent with a perturbed look." My mother had been worrying about it. I told her not to worry, that I'll take care of it, and I immediately had her take salt and incense with both of her hands and bring them near her nose. I asked her to keep doing that for a minute, then remembered something. "Oh yeah, when you're possessed by a cosmic spirit, your own symptoms can be withheld." My mother hurriedly let go of the incense and said "Then no thanks. I'd rather stink than go through that pain." But it was too late. She no longer had the odor. She had a complex expression on her, like she was simultaneously glad and regretful, but there was nothing to worry. After that there was no longer any problem with the odor, her cholangitis, or her fracture. At the hospital we were told that she will have to be constantly lying down inside of a nursing home, so we had made an application for her to enter one, except now it was not necessary. She is now 84 years old, leading a healthy life on her own.

Through this experience I was able to realize once more the greatness of Nomura sensei's studies. I, a normal human being, was able to rescue my mother, and it is a good thing to help your own parent. I am so thankful. I hope people who have concerns about their issues can learn about this and experience it for themselves. Also, the methods that are there now are thousands of times better than before, so the ones learning now are truly fortunate.

Hands that turned bright yellow and the inability to stop eating snacks (Nagoya City/45 years old/female)

I would like to talk about a wonderful experience that I had from the time that I came to learn about waves.

About 4 years ago, I had my blood tested because the palms of both of my hands had turned extremely yellow. However, the test results came out normal. There was no diagnosis and no medication prescribed. And of course, my hands were still bright yellow.

It was then that I went to a session of the School of Waves organized by Nomura sensei, upon being introduced to it by a friend. The people there immediately noticed my hands being extremely yellow, and Nomura sensei made a measurement using the wave measurement device. The result was "hepatitis C."

From general knowledge, I had thought that jaundice was due to a sick liver, but the blood test came out normal, so I didn't know what to do. But the waves said that it was hepatitis C. After that I kept on purifying it with the method that was taught to me. Within a few months, the yellowness disappeared. Nomura sensei had taken a picture of the hands when they were yellow, and the difference was obvious. I was truly surprised. If it had been left alone, I'm sure that the condition would have become worse and I would have become seriously sick. This is not the only time I was saved by Nomura sensei's waves.

There was a time when the sole of my foot was hurting, so I had to wrap a towel around it as I lived my every life. The foot was not swollen and it did not have any visible injury, so I did not know what to do. The measurements said that it was cancer. I purified it using the same method, and on that day I no longer needed a towel because the pain was gone.

There was another time when my stomach was in great pain. My stomach and the area around my stomach was all hurting, like there was something stuck, making it difficult to breathe. I couldn't even stay asleep at night. I asked Nomura sensei to give me a measurement, and she said that a vengeful soul had possessed me. I was in a lot of pain, so I had Nomura sensei purify it for me. She took a picture from various angles, and as she purified it the pain faded away gradually. Within an hour the pain was gone and I could breathe. It was unbelievable that breathing felt so easy. It was hard before, but whatever that was stuck was now gone, and it even felt as if I could breathe too much.

Finally, I would like to talk about the blood test at the Wave Medicine Research Center. At this place, trace amounts of blood are studied using a microscope. Then a picture would be taken and the waves measured.

In my blood there was a large quantity of bacteria and viruses that were causing hepatitis C, swine germs , indigestion, and uterine cancer, which were some of the things that I had had in my life. Subjective symptoms such as pain and throbbing appear to the surface, but they actually exist in the blood in the first place, circulating the body. If a great quantity can be observed from a trace amount of blood, then that means that there is an astronomical number of bacteria and viruses in the blood vessel. It is clear that they are causing illness and any bad condition. It would be better to become healthy by getting rid of them.

I had also suffered from fatigue and eczema, but through the process of purification upon measurement, they have been mitigated and improved. There have been cases where the problem became solved completely.

Not only physical conditions, but mental conditions and personality can be improved as well.

Now I live day by day purifying. In between household chores and work, I take pictures and purify. This routine is a must. I don't think anybody can be happy unless they are healthy.

After learning about Nomura sensei's waves, I have become healthier and healthier, and I am thankful for it.

(As it was noted, this person had come with bright yellow hands. It should be obvious that her problem is jaundice, but the hospital failed to give her the diagnosis. We were first using salt to help purify her, but no matter from what angle I took the picture, the result came out as hepatitis C. The wave measurement device said so over and over. I thought it was strange to not suggest that another test should be made, because it was so obvious what it was even without testing.)

(It was fortunate that she was not prescribed any medication. There's so much to write and I can't write about everything, as it is written in the title of this section, she had been unable to keep herself from eating snacks when she was a child. The garbage can was filled with wrappers every day, and she would still want to eat snacks even though she felt like throwing up. I studied where she was experiencing terrible throbbing, and found a pig with indigestion, uterine cancer, and throbbing. In the blood that we extracted from her we found pig after pig after pig, it being the majority of what we found. We even laughed at one point when we found that her blood looked just like a pig. Because the pig has indigestion, she did not become obese, but her stomach felt heavy. Currently, the thing that bothers her the most is the throbbing that occurs where the pig had appeared, and she is struggling every day. She has been able to improve many conditions before, so she is moving forward with confidence.)

The cause of a week-long tooth ache within the ear (Toyota City/45 years old/male)

About 15 years ago I had been going for the 1st place in a national swimming competition, but suddenly my shoulders, knees, and elbows became inflamed. I was unable to move, and felt at a loss. The cause could not be found at the hospital, but my friend told me about waves, and thinking I had nothing to lose, I went ahead and had an examination. It turned out to be rheumatism, and that time I was given a magnetic necklace with high waves, being able to improve my condition by continuing to wearing it. After a few years I made a complete recovery, and this helped me believe the existence of waves. The necklace was expensive, but I bought several, even giving them to my parents.

Later, I was introduced to Nomura sensei who was doing research about waves, and I consulted her many times about any illness that I had. Even illnesses where the cause was unknown through common methods were cured without the use of any medication. The method itself made progress, and I experienced the immediate amelioration of symptoms that would have taken years before, and I have become surprised continually throughout this progress. Just by placing an amulet with much higher waves than the necklace on the affected part or a picture purify any virus, bacteria, or spirit immediately. I think this would be unbelievable for any person who has only heard of Nomura sensei for the first time.

The next experience I would like to talk about is a toothache.

I am an athlete, so naturally I take care of my health. Even regarding my teeth, if I feel a lack of balance when I am biting or chewing, it will affect the balance of my body. I had the experience previously that this can result to less power, so I had become careful about it. I thought that bruxism occurred due to lack of balance, so I had been having the crown of my teeth adjusted sometimes.

This year, one day my wisdom tooth suddenly began to hurt. It was a dull, heavy pain. At once I tried placing the amulet given to me by Nomura sensei which had high waves, but it didn't work, so I thought that the pain wasn't due to bacteria or viruses.

Next, I thought that my gums had become inflamed because of me clenching my teeth, because I had had a similar pain from doing so in the past.

I checked my teeth, but I didn't feel any awkwardness in the height of any of them, so I went to sleep putting the same mouthpiece that I had used before, so that I won't clench my teeth. However, the next day the pain had not subsided.

I thought that the inflammation had gone bad, so I went to the dentist that I always go to. Somehow, even though an

X-ray was taken, the dentist said there was no problem, and I was just given some painkillers. But I knew that pills can sometimes cause problems because of what's contained in them, so I didn't want to take them.

I decided to talk to Nomura sensei and have her measure me with the wave measurement device. We found out that the cause was not the teeth or gums, but in fact that there was something deep inside the ear. I wasn't able to tell that there was anything wrong with the ear, so I was very surprised. Even the amulet was unable to get rid of it because it was too strong.

But Nomura sensei had impressively innovated her amulet. It evolved so that it possessed greater waves. I tried purifying myself with it, and the pain subsided right then.

The dentist had not ever said that the cause could be anything other than my teeth or gums, and I was only told to take the painkillers. Not only that, but we measured the painkillers with the wave measurement device just in case, and it turned out that because it was a bit contaminated, if I had taken them I would have possibly ended up having other symptoms as well.

I knew that people who do not know about Nomura sensei's wave measurement device would end up taking medication, so I felt sorry for them, and again felt thankful towards Nomura sensei.

I hope that more people will come to a better understanding by learning about my experience.

(This person is a global athlete, who won three medals, gold, gold, and silver, in the previous Masters swimming competition.)

Life after resurrection from being a drugged corpse (Nagoya City resident/51 years old/female)

A few days ago, I reported to Nomura sensei that I was able to cook stew for the first time in 10 years. The joyfully replied "Isn't that nice!"

I had kidney stones and a panic disorder. Because of this reason, I had to take medication for 15 years, and pills would form a mountain if held in one hand.

The first time I met Nomura sensei was at a session for the School of Waves that is held twice a month. Now I have been going for 5 years.

At first I had been lying in bed all day every day. Naturally I could not do household chores for my family, and my husband would go buy a bento for me to eat. He would also help me get to and back from the session held twice a month. My husband to this day performs this errand for me, and said that the day I went to the session, he saw that my face had become brighter afterwards, which gave him hope. There is a 3 year period where I do not have much memory of. I would just go there and come back, sitting there with the appearance of a person who had just got out of bed.

Afterwards, a great transition occurred. I had been hating myself, wanting to die, with the outbursts of panic going on with no end. It was hard. I was suffering, and terrified. My condition was too much for my family to handle. But then Nomura sensei invited me to her house. I spent 3 days with her, bringing the great amount of medicine that I had been taking with me.

M-san, who had always been coming to the sessions, was also there. We would use the wave measurement device, then place salt (back then we used salt) on the affected part. There was so much work that it felt like it was taking forever. During that time I started having funny sensations around my body, and was cursing because I wasn't feeling well. It was then that I had an amazing experience.

All the contaminants were concentrated in my knee, and it was hard to get them out, like the roots of a large tree. I was going through a panic then, and was suffering so much that I was crying and screaming, wishing for death. I said "That's it, I give up," and decided that I'll just keep taking my medication. Then Nomura sensei said to M-san "Should I cut it with light?" and did something with her hand so that light was released from it towards my knee. The roots became severed, and the contaminants left my knee. The panic also ceased.

This was a turning point for me.

Later, Nomura sensei studied the medication I had been taking in detail and made a chart. This solved the mystery. I originally had a kidney stone and panic disorder, but the medication I had been taking over the years had been affecting my head, particularly towards cerebral infarction, dementia, and the hippocampus. We also realized that a lot of the medication contained bacteria, viruses, and spirits. The medication that I was taking initially, antidepressants, medication to suppress panic attacks, and panic stabilizers had influenced me negatively so that I also needed medication for my thyroid gland, high blood pressure, cholesterol, and painkillers. As I had continued taking these medicines, I began having problems in the kidneys, heart, bladder, urinal tract, thyroid gland, rectum, high blood pressure, pneumonia, dizziness, nausea, lethargy, fatigue, anxiety, fear…I had trouble everywhere in my body.

Nomura sensei would use the wave measurement device, and for example would say "Today you are having a problem with your bladder, so it must be hard going to the bathroom," and get rid of the problem. I would then go to the bathroom, and feel refreshed, not being bothered by any feeling like I still had urine in my bladder leftover. The cause would always be revealed, and I would become relieved like magic.

With time progressing like so, from last year the Card of Hikari came to be, which was a great evolution, also being extremely easy to use, which makes me grateful as if I was in heaven.

I became more emotional, and had hope because of Nomura sensei. I was also taught how to think positively. I only have great gratitude. Thank you Nomura sensei.

(I had a phone call from her the other day because she had fallen in to a situation that she could not handle. Being close to tears, she explained that she did not know what to do about her nausea, chills, and pain. I instructed her to send me a photo. I saw that there was a cosmic spirit with the symptoms she said she had: nausea and chills. But along with those the spirit was in fear. There was also a panicking dog. With all the fear and panicking, it was natural that she felt at a loss. Ovarian cancer was also part of the pain. Regarding the cosmic spirit, there was no spine so I could not study it, but it told me itself what its symptoms were. (When the persimmon leaves around my house had started to die, it was because of a cosmic spirit, but we could tell it was fever disease from the symptoms of the leaves. The gardener said that this symptom was spreading, and that chemicals wouldn't work. In my house we were able to fix the problem.)

This time, I decided that I would like to inquire to the gods. The idea was to have the goddess who was with her to come here directly, since she couldn't drive a car. I was driven to do this, because of my personality. I called her and said that that's what I intend to do, and proceeded. The goddess arrived immediately, and when I asked if she was suffering because of a cosmic spirit, the answer was that she indeed was.

I asked where the cosmic spirit came from, and the answer was that it was inside food, and that anybody who ate this food would suffer the same way.

I asked when this matter will settle, and the answer was that it was up to her effort.

I asked the goddess since when she had been accompanying her, and the goddess answered that she had been with her ever since she developed ties in Okazaki.

The goddess said that she was born with the mission of spreading word about the truth of many misfortunes.

There are those like her where a god comes to accompany them during their life. Her daughter was accompanied by a Kannon-sama previously, but now there is no god around her. Apparently her personality went sour and she hadn't been home in 2 years.

So gods choose who to oversee and who to let go of. I hope that we can all possess a kind of mindset where a god would not forget about you.)

The experience of a complete purification even from a long distance (Nagoya City/50 years old/female)

Every day I thought to myself why there is disease in the world. I always wished to have a healthy body. When I was 30 years old, I became diagnosed with chronic thyroiditis, and have taken medication for it for more than 10 years.

Because of my sickness I would get tired easily, or it would be hard to wake up in the morning, and I wondered why this had to happen to me.

At the hospital I was told that I must take medication for my thyroiditis until I die, that it could not be cured. However, I could not give up. I knew that continuing taking the medicine from the hospital will never cure my illness. It was also a fact, though, that I did not know any other way.

Then in my late 40s, I started getting hot flashes, which is said to be a symptom of menopause. It was then that I began to strongly desire for a way to be truly healthy. I feel that it was the guidance of God that I coincidentally met Nomura sensei.

Of course, I had not known about the Card of Hikari at all, so I just thought it was interesting that they were putting something like a card on top of pictures. It gave me a strong impression.

One day when I wasn't feeling well, I started having coughs like asthma where medicine from a hospital couldn't help it. It wouldn't stop, and I couldn't even sleep at night. I was really suffering, and the next day I called Nomura sensei with tears coming to my eyes, explaining that I couldn't do anything about my coughing, and that not even medicine from the hospital would work. It had been just a little while since I began happily participating in the sessions of the School of Waves.

"If you're suffering that much, then please take a picture of your throat and your forehead and send it by email," she said with kindness. I thought that she must be a god or Buddha, and send the email with a hurry. A few minutes later, I felt a sensation like my throat was being pulled, and the coughing ceased. This time with tears of joy, I called Nomura sensei who then said "I got rid of it with the Card of Hikari. You had pharyngitis, and that was causing you to cough."

When I was feeling the pulling, that was exactly when Nomura sensei was purifying the picture with the Card of Hikari. I am amazed at the power of being able to have symptoms resolved even though I lived in Nagoya, just by sending a picture. This power can only be understood by a person who experienced it.

I had been coughing like I had asthma for 40 years, and always had a cold all year long every year. When Nomura sensei took away my pharyngitis, I no longer had the symptoms of a cold. Now I no longer take medicine for thyroiditis at all, and it is my daily routine to place the Card of Hikari on my picture. After meeting Nomura sensei, I feel my health getting better and better. I thank God and Nomura sensei. I am filled with gratefulness every day.

An intractable disease found only in 3 patients in the world, including 1 in Japan, easily cured (Chiryu City/56 years old/female)

I had felt that my child slept very deeply ever since a young age.

When the symptoms began to clearly appear, my child was in the later years of elementary school. He wasn't able to wake up in the morning and go to school with the others. His eyes were open but he wasn't conscious. I found out later that this was a symptom of his illness. He was unresponsive, having a glassy look in his eyes, which only made me assume that he was just being rebellious. Our family became concerned about having a child that wouldn't do what he was told.

In junior high school, he was no longer capable of waking up in the morning whatsoever. He was in a club, but the teacher had a rule that the practice would not begin unless everyone was present, so he had to quit the club, because he was disrupting the morning practice.

I wasn't able to tell when he would wake up, so I would dress him while he was unconscious, drag him to the front door, put him on my back and take him to the car. The nurse at the school helped each time. I took him to school like this 3 or 4 times a week, carrying him to the infirmary. I was told that he would usually wake up around the time the 2nd class ended. Once he's awake, he is able to function as if there was nothing wrong. He was hospitalized to receive an examination, but nothing wrong was found, so his symptoms remained a mystery.

Once he began work, he would frequently be unable to wake up, and somebody from his workplace would wake him up for him. He also suffered from dysgeusia, injury, and burns. After about 4 or 5 years, I got a call from his workplace. "No matter what we do he isn't waking up like he used to, so we took him to the hospital," they said. He had slept a full day or a day and a half before, so I wasn't that worried.

It had been a week and he was still asleep. I tried putting on his favorite music beside his ear, and putting wasabi paste beside his nose so he could smell it, but it didn't work. It was the 18th day that he finally woke up. He had lost 6 kilograms, had less muscle, and could not walk as well as he did before.

Three months after he left the hospital, he fell in to sleep again. There were no beds available in the hospital, so I took care of him for a week at home. I had to give him water and food, change diapers, and change his clothes for him. He couldn't do it himself so it was very hard. While I was taking care of him, he responded to sound of the memorial service version of the Pajna-para-mita sutra and suddenly began trying to tear off his own ears, beat his ears with his fists, and bang his head on the floor, so I put out a sound immediately.

I tried the same thing several times, and he would respond to it each time, so I had him looked at by various psychics and fortune tellers, but the cause was unknown. This time it took him 29 days to wake up. His weight went down by 10 kilograms. The doctor in charge said that he was the 3rd person in the world to have this condition, and that it wasn't narcolepsy. The cause of his irregular sleep was unknown. The same thing happened several times, and one time it took 4 days to find him because nobody knew where he had fallen asleep. The police, his brothers, friends, people from his workplace, and even people from my own workplace all searched for him, and I feel that I owe them a lot for their efforts.

It was July last year when I Nomura sensei was introduced to me. My child had fallen asleep. I wasn't quite certain about her methods, but I was willing to try anything to help my child. I went to the hospital with the person who introduced Nomura sensei, took a picture, and brought it to Nomura sensei. There are contaminants in the telencephalon in his head, so let's remove it. She removed the contaminants immediately. She said to bring more data about him if this didn't work, but I was told that he had gotten up the next day. I was very surprised at how soon what Nomura sensei did took effect. This time his irregularly long sleep stopped with the shortest number of days, being 11. At the hospital he was made to stay so they can study the cause of his waking up, but the cause is still unknown.

I am filled with thankfulness towards Nomura sensei who has helped cure one of the intractable diseases of the world. She says that if the contaminants in the telencephalon are purified before they accumulate, the disease can be prevented, and even if the disease did arise again, that it could still be purified immediately. I felt very encouraged by her words. I consider it a treasure that I have met such a wonderful person. I will thank her always.

The discoveries, practices, and problem-solving ability of Nomura Sensei who leads the pathway to the future (food culture journalist/Tokyo prefecture/45 years old/female)

I met Nomura sensei in May of 2010.

I had been affected by a great amount of stress, which existed in my family, since I was a fetus, and though in my teens I was training as an athlete competing in the national tournament, the stressful environment I was in made my skin and immune system weaker. Not only that, but I naturally attracted spirits to my body, and also had been lying in bed sometimes from anemia, and the period would be between 1 to 2 weeks when it was bad.

I became unable to move to the point where I could no longer get out of bed, and I was unable to leave my room. I would lie in bed, and unless either the spirits possessing me would leave me alone or the sickness got better, I would not be able to go anywhere, and 10 days would pass, making me think "My work and life will come to a halt if this goes on," "I need to escape this," "I can't let anyone else run my company" and such. I was in despair, but right then Nomura sensei called me. I thought that she could help me, and I myself have called her many times to seek help.

I was a nutritionist, so I had some strategies against my anemia, but still I was struggling and the condition had become chronic. It is very difficult to improve anemia with supplements, especially beyond a certain degree. All of my siblings had the same problem, so I knew that symptomatic treatment did not work. Even if you increased your absorption through detoxing, you can't attain any results beyond that.

The measurements that Nomura sensei made were a technique that was quite unique compared to other research institutions. The analysis of the spirits, bacteria, and viruses matched by symptoms, and the way she would use a phase-contract microscope to look at magnified images of blood seemed like the work of Kannon-sama. I think that her being a woman with sense and having maternal compassion along with insight adds to the quality of it. This is not subjectivity from having long-term relations with her, and she herself does not have that kind of subjectivity. You can trust her, and even if your feeling towards her is doubtful when you first meet her, you will eventually believe in her.

Years of working hard with research have bared fruit, especially since 2016. From the summer I began to see benefits with myself, and by the beginning of autumn I had stopped lying down all the time. The garbage that kept appearing in my bloodstream (microbes that kept increasing like maggots, invisible enemy spirits, bacteria, and viruses) one day decreased significantly. It was a striking change.

I had had problems with my body for decades...wobbling, being possessed, not being able to get out of bed, my face suddenly changing, having an extreme itch in my eye (I had to go to Thailand and India for work, and after about 20 visits my eye began to itch so badly I could not put on makeup), menstrual pain...but these problems ceased to exist after meeting Nomura sensei.

I've heard that breast milk is equal to blood, and those who were not given breast milk may have had a nanny, or may have been given powder milk. There is a lot of karmic homework inside of breast milk then, for example bacteria and viruses. There are a lot of phrases that have to do with blood such as "chi wa arasoenai" (those with blood ties cannot fight each other), "chi ga sawagu" (my blood is getting excited), and "kotsuniku no arasoi" (conflict of flesh and blood), but I feel that there is a lot of responsibility that one holds in their blood from the action of their ancestors.

The WHO says the health of the soul is an important factor of health. Our souls choose our mothers before we are born, then once we are born, we journey through this 3 dimensional world with the purpose of spiritual evolution with our bodies as our vehicle. And of course the day comes when we part from our bodies and from this world. The method of Nomura sensei also involves having a conversation with this unseen world, and she pursues and searches for answers from many angles. It is a repetition of discovery and amazement.

While I was alive, I have become able to move my body, which makes me very thankful. I also received guidance regarding how to care to my customers in my company as a nutritionist. I'm glad I was able to not give up and follow Nomura sensei. Within my relationship with Nomura sensei, I have experienced doubt, having questions, practice, questing, hypothesizing, practice, results, change, excitement, excitement, and excitement again…there's always excitement. I think that such an endeavor would not continue otherwise.

Also, we were able to be truly honest with one another. I believe that this book is one of the fruits that resulted from having relations with each other. It is a joy to be able to plow, plant seeds, allow leaves to grow, and for there to be the baring of fruit. People are able to know a part of the truth of the universe, being sucked in to a whirlpool of epiphanies, problems being solved, and the path to the future opens up.

If more people realize, the evolution of spirituality and the ways to achieve peaceful resolutions in this world would be able to be imagined. I feel that a new future would arrive for the planet, the environment, and creatures. Because of Nomura sensei's diligence in doing her research, and her womanly sincerity in trying to save lives, her earnestness, inquisitiveness, deep compassion, and objectivity it has all been possible. The need to learn from the past reached its culmination in the 20th century, so we who live in the 21st century must be able to solve problems with wisdom and tolerance. We must steer towards the direction that this planet needs to go. The things that Nomura sensei has realized, the things she has done, and her talent in solving problems will help greatly, and I write this with hopefulness.

(I have recently received a message from this person. The head of the hospital that she goes to every 2 or 3 months looked at the diagnosis I gave and said "Your anemia is better now! Perhaps the medicine worked? Wait, you didn't receive any medicine…did you do something? You used an original method and did something!" She sent me a thank you letter by email with this message.)

My experience

I am 70 years old now. I have forgotten to count how old I am from the time I was in my 50s. I consider myself still young. I had surgery for breast cancer when I was 40, but I have never been to the hospital for decades, not even for an examination.

After learning about waves, I felt that examining myself is a 1000 times more effective, which is a reality, so I have nothing to worry about.

I did have some problems. Since I was a child I had a predisposition of not being able to sweat. I wouldn't be able to metabolize, and when I played sports I would turn red in the face instead. When I came home from volleyball my husband would say to me "the red ogre is back" with a laugh. There were many other metabolic disorders also.

This was also since childhood, but I would suddenly get so sleepy that I would begin to yawn, and this would happen regardless of whether I was studying, working, or driving. It was dangerous because though I tried hard to stay awake while driving while chewing gum with the window open, I would suddenly lose my memory, then almost crash in to the car in front of me. I would use the breaks to prevent the crash, but this has happened several times. The causes that appeared were cerebral infraction, arteriosclerosis, thrombosis, arachnoid, dementia, hippocampus, and Altzeimer's. There was an incredible number of brain diseases. By purifying them each day, I was able to stop having the symptoms. If I hadn't known the truth, I would surely have been hospitalized and bed-ridden for the rest of my life.

Also, this year on March 10th my right wrist began to hurt. My right wrist would hurt ever since I was a child, but it would always get better so I didn't worry about it. However, as I grew older it became very swollen, and it would hurt so much that I could not sleep. It was terrible. The same thing would happen to my left knee, and sometimes I would be unable to walk.

What I did was spend a week purifying it, then get back to my life as if nothing had happened. This time, though, I thought that I must have a conversation so that it will never occur again. But my hand hurt so I could not use the wave measurement device. I didn't know the cause, so I asked someone who could use the machine to come and help, and this person figured out the cause with my instructions. There was a spirit that had a negative reading for pain associated with "sprain" (virus), "ligament" (virus), and "fracture" (bacteria). The spirit was in a lot of pain, because it took a long time for the pain to go away even though I was purifying it. I was in so much pain the night before that I could not do anything about it.

That night, the pain finally subsided by purifying 3 spirits. I still could not hold chopsticks, so I wondered if there was still something there, and I found viruses that were negative for pain in the bones. I had just received a message from the gods that I should talk to bacteria and viruses. The spirit said that the pain could not be relieved easily, but I healed it with God's light and it became better. There was so much pain, so I understood that there was something wrong with my wrist and knee. It took a week to be able to use my wrist. I had a volleyball match after that week, but nobody knows about my truth. The other day, I mistakenly sent a picture of my hand when it was in a bad condition, and the person who received said the she thought it was a cursed photo, which we laughed about.

I also asked the god some questions when I was with a person who knew about waves.

1. **The same symptoms have occurred many times. This one is also the same.**
2. **The increase of pain correlates to the increase of thought.**
3. **Certain people who are possessed do not get better as quickly as most people.**
4. **Like we have taught you before, having a conversation with each soul will cure it.**
5. **There are other methods.**

6. A great evil is behind it.

7. Everyone is suffering something similar.

8. Other

I wrote down these 8 choices and asked the gods their opinion.

The answer was number 7.

I had many choices so I asked again, and again it was number 7.

I thought that the gods would be sympathetic...the two of us agreed that the gods were quite strict.

The answer then had come from 11 gods.

Purification is not easy. You must go through the cleaning yourself without any help. The gods provide the knowledge of the cause of it and the method to remove it. You can say the same thing about the purification of the planet. People must go through the cleaning process by themselves. That is what the gods said, and through this conversation have provided the method in how to do it.

(I knew that I had been accompanied by Kannon-sama since childhood because of a photo. Since 2017 when I began purifying everyone, many gods came to my house, and at the same time they had been coming to me. During the conversation with the Satanic spirit in the Security Council, 30 gods were protecting me. Many gods have come to me since then, and now I am protected by more than 50 gods.

I am very thankful and it is an honor, but even then I still suffer from the sleepiness as before, along with other symptoms such as my eyes getting heavy. When I purify it, I see cosmic spirits. Unless you purify it yourself, nobody will help you. My eldest son was also accompanied by Kannon-sama, but his life ended short after 1 year and 1 month. God does not help.

Currently, because I am able to have conversations with gods, I have become able to receive the benefits of being told the cause, method, and light. However, it is a must for one to help themselves, or for a parent to help their own child. Also, we must all purify the planet and the universe. God will teach, but not do everything for us.

All the things that God wishes to say to us is written down inside this book.

Chapter 6

The Way of Salvation is to Surrender to the Guidance of God

The cause of the Tottori earthquakes

On October 19th 2015, news was being reported that there were several consecutive earthquakes happening in Tottori prefecture. It said that in the past Tottori experienced earthquakes in 1943 and 2000, and this time it was 2015.

On October 19th 2015 the news reported that people were concerned that there were 12 earthquakes within a 5 day period. I thought of the people I knew there, and when I saw images of the location of the epicenter on television, I took a picture of it in a hurry. Epicenters were usually in the ocean, but this time it was on land. I made a measurement.

There were cows that were negative with anger, stress, and nerve tissue, multiplying and increasing in number. They must have been through a hard time. Perhaps the peak of their anger became the earthquake. "I'm so sorry! I'm going to help you now!" I said, and purified them. Their anger disappeared and they went off to the heavens. I called a friend, told her that I had just purified the cows, and asked friend to see if the earthquakes would continue or not, and the earthquakes stopped.

I was looking at a blog that said that there was an earthquake in Tochigi prefecture on April 3rd 2016. The number was about half compared to the time in Tottori, but I saw female horse spirits who were fatigued. I purified their fatigue.

The cause of the Kumamoto earthquake

The television said on April 14th 2016 that there was an earthquake in Kumamoto. I took a picture of the epicenter, and saw animal spirits, this time female horses that were negative with "anger" and "colon." It was 10:30pm, but I wanted to calm the earthquake and help ease the suffering of the horses, so I went ahead with the purification in the midst of the dark outdoors. I took a confirmation photo using a flash, to make sure the purification was done. I thought that the earthquake was calm now, but there was another one on the 15th. I looked at the picture of the epicenter and saw a male horse with anger and a colon problem. It was 7pm, quite late, and I was sleepy, but I felt strongly that the damages need to stop as soon as possible, so I purified it. I thought that I was finished, but on the 16th at 7am, this time there was a female short-tempered and angry pig. I had it ascend to the heavens at 9am.

On the 16th at 7am, there was report of 11 students being buried alive in Minamiasomura. The scene of the event was on television so I took a picture. There was a female bird with stress and throbbing pain. I purified her after 9am.

Afterwards, I found a sorrowful female, an obsessive male with anger and stress, and a short-tempered angry obsessive male, so I purified all of them. On the 18th there was a male horse with vertigo because of neuralgia. On the 21st there was bull with neurological abnormalities, and again on the 21st there was a male bear with anger. I purified all of them.

On the 24th I saw a satellite image of the area around Aso Ohashi. Here, there was a concentration of 1. Male bird with sorrow and neurosis, 2. Male bird with stress and lethargy, 3. Bull with pain in the liver and anger, 4. Male pig with stress and colon problems, 5. Male horse with lethargy.

All of these animals are ones that we use for food regularly.

Birds are divided between male and female. Males become food, and females are forced to lay eggs the rest of their lives.

Pigs, within the first week of their lives, have their teeth forcefully removed, tails cut off, and their genitals ripped off, all without anesthesia. Birds and pigs both are locked up all their lives in a narrow space so that they will be food for humans. We are being very cruel to them. How would you feel if you or your children were treated this way? It's important to think about it. These acts of cruelty will come back to us humans like an echo.

When the earthquake began in Kumamoto, because I had told a member of mine that there are many horses in Kumamoto, she said "Then it must be because of horses! How obvious! Every restaurant in Kumamoto serves horse sashimi!" And the earthquakes indeed were started by horses, male and female. They had been bred for food.

As a prevention of the spreading of avian influenza and

foot-and-mouth disease, in Kyushu tens of thousands of animals were killed and buried, including healthy ones. These animals suffered from anger, stress, lethargy, fatigue, and pain. I feel that the earthquake was a result of a chain reaction that occurred from their spirits being in agony for decades. I asked the Kanzeon Bosatsu-sama who was with me, and I was told that many earthquakes are caused by the anger of animals.

When there is a forecast for rain, there is also the danger of the occurrence of mudslides. Inside of rain and in the eye of typhoons, there are many animal spirits, especially snakes. When a snake is in pain or if it is angry, it becomes quite possible for there to be damages from their power. I paid attention to weather forecasts and purified them as much as I could after taking pictures.

When I had become busy every day from the Kumamoto earthquakes, I was walking with a member of the School of Waves, and she suggested that it might be possible to look at satellite images on the internet. The television would only give satellite maps once in a while, which made the work hard. After attaining this good information, I became able to look all around the world with satellite images. Whenever the television would give a report of a typhoon, I would look at the satellite image of it and purify any spirit, bacteria, or virus that I see. You can even prevent the flue if you could omit the cause of it.

This applies to all earthquakes, typhoons, and hurricanes.

If the prevention can be made so easily, I feel that I should check satellite images of around the world every day. However, currently I am too busy to do that. I would like others to do it themselves once they have the understanding. However, I don't feel it is good to be complacent about how animals are treated now just because someone will always be able to prevent the natural disasters. Animal welfare will have to be thought about carefully, and hopefully in the future we will be able to make food that tastes similar to meat which is not really meat.

The first plea towards dragon gods with Typhoon 18

On September 16th 2017, after the incident of North Korea's missile launch finally settled, the enormous Typhoon 18 arrived to Kyushu. It was reported that it would affect all of Japan. I asked for help again.

I asked the dragon gods, dragons, anacondas, and big snakes to come. I thanked them for having helped with the heavy rain in Kyushu and Typhoon 5.

This time Typhoon 18 is coming, and it is being said that it will affect the whole country. I hope that you can help again.

Today I have found out that 1 dragon, the husband of the anaconda family, the husband of the anaconda couple who were in Oceania, the big snake siblings, and the one who had throbs from the burning in the field, a total of 6, had been in hell. Out of these 6, those who went to hell for the first time must have truly suffered. Half had been there for the 2nd time, and I'm sure they don't want to go back. The anaconda family had been able to become reunited before, but because the father went missing again, the mother and son had felt lonely.

Once they all arrived, I asked them if they could help with Typhoon 18. Perhaps I would also ask the 7 dragon gods that I had talked about the other day.

They said that they would appreciate it if I also asked the 7 dragon gods for help, and went off to the typhoon.

At 4:30 in the afternoon, I called the dragon gods as I promised. It was my first encounter with them, so I didn't know I would actually meet them or not.

One male dragon god and 6 female dragon gods came from Australia.

Question

"I have just now explained the situation. Do you understand?"

Answer

"Yes."

Question

"You are 1 male god and 6 female gods?"

Answer

"That's correct."

Question

"Typhoon 18 is coming to the shores of Kyushu today and it is being said that it will affect the whole archipelago of Japan. I would like to prevent damages from wind and rain as much as possible. Human beings do not have that power and I would like to ask your help."

Answer

"We will do our best."

"We will go assist the others who have gone before us."

They left at 5:16pm from my house.

I looked at the internet, and saw that after the 7 gods departed, they had all assembled at the southeast of Kyushu and the violent wind and rain had changed its direction towards the Japan Sea. There were 10 made up of the dragons, anacondas, and big snakes, with 11 dragon gods behind them. They knew what they were doing, which made me feel secure. Once Typhoon 18 was gone, I was thankful because though it was said to be large, there was not much damage.

On September 19th Tuesday I called everyone over to thank them about Typhoon 18. Before that I wanted to call the 4 bi snakes that were in Hurricane Irma so that the others could meet them.

I told them that I'll call over the ones that helped with Typhoon 18 and that I hoped they could all be friends. Then I called the 11 dragon gods and the 10 others. It was because of their efforts towards Typhoon 18 that the typhoon caused minimal damage between September 16th and September 18th. We all thanked them for it.

Question

"What can you do?"

Answer

"Make the strong winds smaller."

"Create strong winds."

"Change the direction of the wind."

"Move rainclouds."

"Create rainclouds when there is fire."

The 4 big snakes the joined yesterday answered about their abilities.

Question

"Compared to the previous typhoon, this time 7 dragon gods accompanied the efforts. How did everyone feel?"

Answer

"We were glad that many dragon gods could come, it was encouraging." (4 dragon gods, 10 others)

"The typhoon this time was enormous but we were able to pull through." (4 dragon gods, 10 others)

"We saw them in the typhoon, but we are glad to be able to see them again here." (4 dragon gods, 10 others)

"We are also very glad to see them." (the 4 big snakes from Hurricane Irma)

"We are very happy to be able to see these friends today." (7 dragon gods)

With such strong friends who are on our side, it makes me feel secure and happy. I am hopeful towards the future.

They ate 5 eggs, then each went off to where they had come from.

I took a picture of when they departed, and saw that they were in the clouds. I will cherish this picture.

The animals that were in Hurricane Irma

On September 18th Monday there was a typhoon going on in Hokkaido, but Honshu was having clear autumn weather. I had asked the experienced dragon gods to deal with the typhoon, so I was working on something else. That day 2 friends of mine had come to assist me, and we talked about Hurricane Irma and how there were 4 angry snakes and 150 angry cows in it. We decided to ask them what they were doing in there.

Question

"Am I talking to those who were in the great Hurricane Irma on September 10th?"

Answer

"Yes." (150 female cows, 4 snakes)

"We were treated very poorly by humans and became

angry." (150 female cows)

"We were in the hurricane, trying to make it bigger so that we could have revenge against humans." (4 snakes)

"The humans forced us to have babies and then took them away." (150 female cows)

"They had us shown for entertainment in a zoo." (4 snakes)

"We went to the hurricane and our anger exploded inside it." (4 snakes)

Question

"It seems that you were not eating, but why?"

Answer

"We felt nauseated and ill in general." (4 snakes)

"We were so angry that we did not feel like eating." (150 female cows)

They really did go through a hard time. Humans tend to only think of themselves, but I hope that we will be able to think about animals more. In this book that is going to be published, I will write about you. I will make a plea for animal welfare and hopefully many people will come to a realization.

Question

"How is your anger, and how do you feel in general?"

Answer

"Much better." (all)

I told them to please eat and be well, and we parted.

A lot of animals in a lot of places are being treated poorly. I wish people would put themselves in their situation and think "What if I was an animal?" I think that people who treat animals poorly will most likely become an animal in their next life. People must train their minds to be able to understand animals. Out of the many conversations I've had, I have had may encounters where the animal spirit said it was formerly human. Then they finally realize why they became an animal. It is only about 80 years to be human, but in the spiritual world one is haunted with the reality of being an animal for hundreds of years. I certainly hope that justice will be done.

Various events that occurred along with Typhoon 22 (Oct. 27th, 2017)

I heard the news that Typhoon 22 changed its course and went southward, meaning that it did not go across the Japanese archipelago. It made me think of the dragon gods that I have been asking to assist with typhoon damage control.

I immediately looked at satellite images. All of the 11 dragon gods, along with 14 others, who helped with Typhoon 21 were there. I hesitated to ask for help again, because I thought I was asking them too much. However I was able to confirm that the gods were in line together going from the archipelago towards the Pacific Ocean. They had used their power.

There were 80 angry snakes, 12 spirits with diarrhea, and

77 dogs damaged by drugs. When I called them to thank them before, they had said that it's better to not have anything in the typhoon, so I called the animals who were there to have a conversation.

The spirits with diarrhea had passed away because of food poisoning as a group. The dogs damaged by drugs had died from an infectious disease.

The angry snakes had been drugged to death in China, and they had been making the typhoon worse that in already was in order to have revenge. I saw that there were actually many snakes with their mouth wide open in the typhoon.

I also saw images of cute dogs, ones that had been damaged by drugs.

The angry snakes felt better after I removed their harm from drugs, so I asked them to go help the dragon gods with the typhoon. I asked the others to go back to their places of birth.

The nuclear threat from North Korea, defeated by the power of God!

In 2017 North Korea had become a world issue. Nuclear weapons were part of it, and involved the environment and the rest of the world, so the whole world was paying attention.

As I wrote in Chapter 2, I have been purifying anything

radical that I notice such as Satanic spirits, spirits with neurological abnormalities, hysterical spirits, or animal spirits. I can see radiation around the world using the internet, so when I found radiation in North Korea, I had always been purifying it. There would always be a news report saying that a missile launch failed, and I knew that it was connected to the purifications.

North Korea said that it would launch 4 missiles to Guam on August 9th, and I saw on the internet a missile being placed on a launchpad on the 10th, 11th 12th, and 13th. It was really happening, but they were all purified so I told everyone that it's okay. On August 26th, it was reported that 3 missile launches failed. On the 29th, there was a report that 1 launch was successful. The missile went over Hokkaido and crashed in to the Pacific Ocean.

Because they had launched so many missiles, I wondered if there was more, so on August 30th I called the spirit group from North Korea that I had called before which consisted of 38 spirits.

Question

"After being here on April 6th, what did you do?"

Answer

"We went back to North Korea."

"We are also being careful about Kim Jung-eun."

"On August 26th they launched 3 missiles, and they cancelled the 4th one because the others failed."

"He is unleashing his anger on the manufacturers of the missiles because they failed."

"These missiles were launched towards Guam."

"They thought the 4th launch would work because they made a repair."

"It was the last missile. There won't be any more."

"They don't have the resources or financial capabilities for more launches."

"They keep plutonium underground."

"There is still 1 nuclear missile."

"They want to launch it to the United States."

"They also were targeting the United States with the 4 launches."

"For North Korea to become peaceful, ○○○○○ would be the best thing to happen."

Recently, there was a report that Mr. Kim was inspecting a hydrogen bomb, and he was making bold comments. Afterwards, I was looking in the internet and saw the 1 nuclear missile that they had on September 1st at 11am. I purified it right away. Another one came up on September 3rd at 8am. I wondered how that could be, because based on the information from the other day there should have been only 1 left. I called the 38 spirits, and they explained.

Answer

"It's because they repaired the other missile yesterday."

"This time it's nuclear."

"They're thinking of doing it on the 9th Sunday, their national foundation day."

"If you purify it, they'll just repair it, so better purify it on the 8th."

"They want to shoot a missile towards Guam."

"They haven't loaded the nuclear materials yet."

"They just want to show off their power for self-gratification."

Question

"Wouldn't that cause a world war?"

Answer

"Kim thinks he can survive a world war."

"He has an underground shelter just in case."

"They do expect the United States to strike back."

Question

"Don't the people of North Korea understand these things through foreign media?"

Answer

"They are too brainwashed to understand."

Question

"There was an announcement made the other day that journalists who write blasphemous things about North Korea will be killed. Have assassins been sent? How many people are involved?"

Answer

"An order of that kind has been made."

"More than 6 people."

Question

"How many children does Mr. Kim have? Their gender?"

Answer

"Three."

"They're all male."

During the conversation, I heard the news that there had been a nuclear test. On September 4th I made a measurement of negative 50 for radiation, plutonium, and cesium at the place where the nuclear test was made. On September 7th Thursday 11:45am, I asked the 38 spirits to come over and heard about what's been going on.

Answer

"There are no changes in the plan to launch a missile towards Guam on the 9th. It is scheduled to be launched around noontime on the 9th."

"They haven't loaded the nuclear material yet."

"They are going to confirm that they've been able to maintain the ability of the plutonium."

"The confirmation will be done tomorrow afternoon."

"They will inspect the place that they had a failure on

September 9th 10am."

"If there is an abnormality in the inspection tomorrow, they will not know whether the launch will be done."

At 8:15pm the 8th the next day, I had the 38 spirits from North Korea come and tell me the results.

Answer

"They made the inspection for plutonium as scheduled, in the afternoon."

"There were abnormalities."

"There is no explosive power."

"They want to add something that would have explosive power."

"They want to be ready by the 9th."

"They are repairing."

"Plutonium is what has explosive power."

"That's why they're thinking of doing repairs."

"They're finished with that for the day, and are preparing for tomorrow."

"Tomorrow they will launch after having an inspection with the place that there is always a failure."

"Tomorrow at 10am, we will figure out if there is change in plans or not, and you can decide whether to purify or not."

I checked the internet, and there was plutonium with a measurement of positive 20 that didn't exist September 8th 7:30pm, but somehow did after an hour. It must be something they wish to have in the missile for its strong effects. The next day, on the 9th at 10:20am, another thing became clear from talking to the 38 spirits.

Answer

"They added plutonium yesterday to make the missile stronger, and they think it's a success."

"The inspection here is probably finished."

"The scheduled time is 1pm."

"The purification should be done at 12pm."

I was told to do the purification at 12pm, but for some reason I made a mistake and did it at 11am. There was no discovery made that it was me who had purified the missile along with the plutonium that was inside it.

However, at 3pm I detected radiation again as usual. If the launch was 4pm that would mean trouble. I didn't have time to call anyone over, so I began purifying right away. Afterwards, nothing happened, so I called 19 spirits over at 4:30pm. I called over half of them so that the other half can stay in North Korea in case anything would happen there.

Question

"It seems that the launch hasn't happened yet. Have changes occurred because of the purification? What time is it being scheduled?"

Answer

"It is scheduled to be done within the day."

"6pm."

Question

"I purified the missile at 4pm, but will this be discovered again?"

Answer

"It is hard to say."

I thought that if the launch would occur at 6pm, then it would be safe because the purification was done. But the launch was delayed. At 9:20pm I called the 19 spirits over again.

Question

"The malfunction was detected. They were not able to repair it and it became 8:30pm, where then the repair was done using a different kind of substance. What do you think?"

Answer

"Where it was radiation before, they changed to plutonium."

"It is scheduled for 11pm tonight."

"They really want to launch it on their national foundation day."

"They have become very careful. They may do an inspection around 11:30pm."

"Kim is screaming at people."

"It would be best to do the purification right at 11:30."

"If you do things that way today it will be good."

The launch on September 9th was cancelled. The next day on the 10th, I had the 19 spirits come to me at 11:45 am.

Question

"Sorry to trouble you by having you come here so many times. The purification was done at 11:30 yesterday. The launch seems to have been cancelled, but why?"

"They detected the usual malfunction."

"They are unable to repair it, and cannot schedule another launch."

"They want to launch no matter what, and are working harder than ever on repairing."

On 2:50pm on September 11th I called the 19 spirits over to ask about what's going on.

"They've been busy with repairing since then."

"They are making parts."

"They have no idea when they will be finished."

"Kim is frustrated and shouting at people."

"He is ordering people to get it fixed right away."

"They're thinking of doing another launch soon after getting it fixed."

"Today, representatives from a countries around the world are getting together to discuss what to do about North Korea's threats, and North Korea is concerned."

"If they get frustrated, they're gonna want to launch a missile."

"Either way, they'd really like to show off their power."

"Resources like oil and food are decreasing. Oil will especially become a problem."

Question

"If I purify it after the repair, do you think that they will find the malfunction again and try to repair it?"

Answer

"Timing is very important."

"Perhaps 5 minutes before the launch would be good."

On September 12th at 5:45pm I had a conversation again with the 19 spirits.

Question

"Judging from what I see with the internet, it seems that they haven't repaired it yet."

Answer

"It will be finished soon."

"They didn't like the decision of the Security Council this morning, and are angry."

When I had them come, it seemed that the repair was finished, based on what I saw on the internet. I hurriedly did the purification at 6:15. The missile would not launch. The spirits gave these answers:

Answer

"They may have discovered it."

"They have more parts so they can make another one."

"If they discover the malfunction, they will just begin making another one."

On September 13th 12:13pm, I had a conversation with the 19 spirits.

Question

"The launch would not happen, so I was wondering what was going on?"

Answer

"It is another malfunction."

"They're going to do it differently this time."

"They're going to be using the same part."

"They would like to launch it right after the repair."

"Day or night does not matter."

"People will report the completion of the repair to Kim, who then will choose the time."

I checked the internet during the conversation and found radiation and plutonium. As the 19 spirits had said, it seemed that they had changed their methods. They had decided to use 2 types of materials this time.

Question

"Was the repair completed after that?"

Answer

"Not yet. It will still take time."

I had everyone go back for now, and decided to have them what time the launch will be. At a little before 2pm, I called 19 spirits, half of their total number.

Answer

"There will be no launch at 2pm."

"It will be after 3 o'clock."

At 3:18pm, I talked with the 19 spirits.

Answer

"The repair is finished."

"The launch will be at 4 o'clock."

"Please purify it around the same time, at 4 o'clock."

However, the launch did not occur at 4pm. At 6:17pm, I talked to the 19 spirits.

Question

"I purified it at 4pm, so what happened?"

Answer

"The button was not pushed at 4 o'clock."

"There are still more parts."

"There're going to check again before the launch so they will find out."

"Perhaps Kim hesitated because it was the last missile which he needed to take care of."

"Perhaps he will give orders once he is in a bad mood."

On this day I had the 2 groups of 19 spirits each come 5 times, so I gave them my apologies and thanked them. I didn't want the purification on September 13th to be found out, so I waited until the last minute to do it. When I thought that this time would become a success, they hesitated. If they delay it, they will find out it was purified and repair it.

There was no radiation on September 14th, so I thought that the missile had not been repaired. I started doing my work in the evening which had been piling up, and was in front of the computer until 4am. I slept a little past 4am and got up at 8am, where then I received a phone call with the message that North Korea had finally launched a missile. At 10:45am, after the launch, I called the 38 spirits from North Korea.

Question

"So they have finally launched. Please tell me what you know."

Answer

"The repaired without using the nuclear material they usually use."

"They were thinking of a mushroom cloud forming in the ocean."

"They wanted to show the explosion to threaten the world."

"But there was no explosion, so they're questioning the manufacturer angrily."

"If there had been a nuclear explosion, they would have been broadcasting the video of it with pride."

"The manufacturers are also worried because it didn't go well."

"Now there are no missiles, no nuclear materials, no money

to finance it, all ruined for them."

"They are thinking about how to deal with the sanctions they are receiving from other nations which will put their people in a crisis."

"They will keep telling the world that they still possess power and will not admit their defeat."

"They will hide whatever they can hide."

"They tell the citizens of their country only the good sides of things."

"They want to prevent riots."

Question

"On the 14th, nuclear material after a repair was not detected from the internet, which was unusual. I thought that they were just unable to repair it. I made a confirmation just now and found out that they had fixed it using another way. Were you thinking of contacting me about this?"

Answer

"We thought it would be no use because it was a different method. Our mindset was 'oh well.'"

"The nuclear material was purified, and the missile was directed towards the ocean, so we were not worried."

Question

"I see that they chose the ocean because that would prevent the worst scenario, that the United States would attack them. But what action will Kim take, knowing that all of his attempts failed because of purification?"

Answer

"He will know the power of God."

"We have done what we can."

"I think that he is going to keep being self-centered, and that he would like to keep his authority."

"Please say in your next book that nobody can defeat the power of God."

I called the 38 spirits from North Korea every day and attained much information. In the end the missile had been launched in to the ocean, with the ocean not being polluted by the nuclear material. I am very thankful. If they had launched a missile to Guam, not only would there have been much damage, but it could have developed in to a war. I think it was the best path based on our circumstances. This is all because of God and because of the help of others. I gave thanks to the gods and gave them a report.

With the light of God, the greatest danger in the world, nuclear weapons, has disappeared. The missiles also could not be launched. All the money that came from the hard work of people became nothing in a flash. People around the world should know that military power is meaningless. They should know that we are now in the age of God.

On September 24th 2017, 9 days after the launch of a nuclear missile, I had another conversation with the 38 spirits from

North Korea.

Question

"Kim is threatening the world that he will conduct tests with hydrogen bombs, but does he really have this capability?"

Answer

"There's nothing left that would make that possible."

"People are agreeing upon this fact."

"The administrators and the missile manufacturers know there's nothing."

"They are putting on a false front that does not reflect the truth about their ability."

"The citizens do not know."

Question

"Yesterday (September 23rd) there was an earthquake there, wasn't there?"

Answer

"It happened many kilometers away from the nuclear experiment."

"It was a natural earthquake, not an experiment."

"The ground became weak from the previous experiment."

"There are casualties and some destruction of buildings."

Question

"Sanctions are being talked about in the world, but how does Kim feel?"

"The sanctions are becoming more and more severe, and it

is making him frustrated."

"He is taking out his stress on others."

"From here on, he will make arguments with words, but will be unable to use military force."

"If North Korea experienced at military raid, they would not be able to retaliate."

"If they were to fight on home ground, they would use tanks and machine guns."

Question

"I have just now read aloud the section from my book to be published entitled 'The nuclear threat from North Korea, defeated by the power of God!' What do you think?"

Answer

"It's all true."

"We hope that this sequence of events will be revealed to the world, and they will come to understand that military force is meaningless."

Answer

"We're glad we were able to assist from the spiritual side of things."

"When later this information comes in to the ears of the manufacturers of the missiles, they will acknowledge it."

"If the manufacturers acknowledge it, so will Kim."

The entire world is discussing the issue of North Korea and nuclear weapons. I have been able to bring the results of removing the frightening possibility of North Korea's nuclear capabilities. They performed the role of the villain and conducted the nuclear tests which nobody would have wanted to do, and this resulted in people knowing that you cannot defeat the power of God. These events support the fact that the existence of God is a reality. If Earth becomes peaceful, that would mean that North Korea contributed to it.

I hope that the world and North Korea can get over any obstacle with their hands together.

[New Information: discovery of nuclear cells that could destroy humanity!]

There was a woman who was at the brink of death but came back to life because of purification. As I was moving forward with the publication of this book, she contacted me.

Again, she had become uncomfortable with nausea, diarrhea, and frequent urinating. She said that she had been purifying herself but the problems had kept haunting her and she needed help. Because she was eating food after purifying it thoroughly, I didn't think it would be probable that her problems came from the food she ate.

I had her come the evening before the session for the School of Waves, and I studied her condition. There was nausea, diarrhea, frequent urinating, and discomfort, which I cleansed with salt. There were things that came out from other members that day, I had a conversation with all of them at once. As always, I started with classification. I had whatever that was there choose what it was through multiple choice.

1. I am a spirit.

2. I am bacteria.

3. I am a virus.

4. I am a cosmic spirit.

5. I am bacteria that was cultivated by people.

6. Other

I added number 5 on list this day wondering with suspense that it would be valid. Three of them were viruses, 8 of them were cosmic spirits from the planet of Himorowaroyorarunnya, and 31 of them were bacteria cultivated by people!

I became frightened, realizing the horror of the situation. Also, thought the viruses and cosmic spirits would say that they felt better after their purification, the bacteria cultivated by people would say that they still felt bad. I realized that it takes longer for them to get better.

After the realization, I have added "I am cultivated bacteria with genetic engineering" to the list to have them choose it. Without this on the list previously, I have encountered "other" as an answer many times, which turned out to be Cell (there is no name so I am calling it " Cell.") I used to think that it is very hard dealing with the number of cosmic spirits, but now I know that there are more Cells. Incredible.

They are rather smart, knowing their circumstances quite well, and they answer thoroughly. As I studied this I came to horrifying discoveries. It is very hard to study Cell. Similar to cosmic spirits, they have no spine, and along with that they have no gender differentiation. I have to input the symptom itself and the phase of that symptom to get a response. For example, just with vomiting it is plus 0 ~ plus 90 or minus 0 ~ 90 meaning that I must make about 20 measurements to find out what phase it is.

The woman with the vomiting had the measurement of plus 50, and this came from the tea she had been drinking for the past 6 months without purifying it. I went and bought the tea so that I can examine it, and found 5 Cells in it causing the vomiting. She had been drinking it for 6 months so this was terrible, and she really needed purification so that she will stop being nauseated.

These Cells answered the question "What were you inside of?" Medicine, health products, beverages, and also I wrote down names of items that I remembered having, and they would answer. Recently I have many conversations with the Cells that were in the woman's body, and they say honestly that they were in the tea she was drinking, same as before.

The pills for constipation that she had been taking 20 years before had caused frequent urination and discomfort, and she has been suffering for more than 20 years. However the Cells have answered exactly what the cause was. Through the testament of Cells, we have found out that what the woman had been drinking for her health has actually not been healthy.

If Cell carries symptoms, the same symptom will come to the host. However, there are those who are sensitive to it and those who are not so sensitive to it. Whatever the case, it should be spotted and purified as soon as possible, but the world still does not know about this, and hospitals interpret certain symptoms as just having an unknown cause or that it is due to the nature of the patient. I can only say that I feel sorry for those who cannot purify.

These are the things the Cells told me through conversation:

1. **We don't know what we shout do from hereon.**
2. **We wish we were never born.**
3. **We wish we were never created.**
4. **We were probably created in order to benefit human beings, but our existence doesn't really benefit anyone, just causes suffering.**

They all chose number 4. After seeing this response, I was overwhelmed with tears. No apology could make up for this. The only way to help the Cells would be to stop the manufacturing as soon as possible. The list made by the Cells who appeared within the past few days is composed of lethargy (health products), neurological abnormalities (medicine, health products), pain (health products), the entire brain (tea, etc.), anemia (health products), obesity/vomiting (health products), and diarrhea (medicine, tea). People with these symptoms should see if the health products and medicine they are taking are okay.

Children and young people are now having symptoms that were unthinkable in the past such as allergies, hay fever, decrease in vision, and lethargy. It is because they have been surrounded by foods that cause them since birth, and have become defected by it. There are too many Cells inside these products. It is a horrifying situation.

This is a problem that must be faced by all citizens of the world. This problem will cause many damages in developed nations. It was good that the problem was detected before it could spread to developing nations. People of developed nations will probably be able to solve their own problem with their own efforts. Japan is God's nation. I hope Japan can stand at the forefront and show others how everything should be accomplished. I asked the gods:

Question

"I am astounded by the revelation of the cultivated bacteria. What should be done?"

Answer

"Purify as usual."

"If you don't stop it, terrible things will happen."

"These bacteria were cultivated through genetic engineering."

"When they enter the human body, the person will develop mental and physical abnormalities."

The next day I got out the things I had in my house that I was using and took a look at them. There were a lot of Cells in them. Food products that were labeled with statements declaring that genetic engineering had not been done had 17 Cells in them. These Cells were bad for the pharynx and bronchial tubes, so I figured out that it was the reason I had been having problems with my pharynx.

I looked in to the condition of one of my family members, and she had been eating snacks containing many Cells (8 in one bag). This had been why her uterus hurt since she was young, why she was always sleepy, why she had no energy, and why she experienced throbs. Because things were going wrong around my own environment, I decided to inquire the gods again.

Answer

"Genetic engineering should not be done."

"There are only negative consequences for humanity."

"Genes were created by God."

"Genetic engineering creates negative cells, and they are a negative influence on human beings."

"As a result, it brings about cancer, allergies, hay fever, and diseases where the cause is unknown."

"Cells have a mind of their own."

"Only the Card of Hikari can purify it."

"A Cell that was purified with a Card of Hikari will wander about, and when food is eaten they will enter someone's body."

Question

"The Cells said they wish they were never born. Is there a way to have them disappear with no pain?"

Answer

"They will eventually be gone if you put them on top of the Card of Hikari."

When I heard this, it eased my tension. I asked about what to do from hereon.

Answer

"Demand for types with no genetic engineering, and create an industry that makes better products."

"Teach at hospitals how to remove Cells, bacteria, viruses, cosmic spirits, and damages due drugs, which have affected people and animals, by themselves."

If people can look at these facts positively, that they were glad to know it, then I feel that people can come up with more wonderful methods.

Message from Amaterasuoomikami-sama: "Re-e-ta-ki-ru-na-ke-i-a-a-ya-fu-ha-sa"

I was hurrying with the publication of "A New World With God!", trying to get it done within the year. I have also published 2 books in the past. Tama Publishing came and introduced themselves to me first.

My wish was for them to experience having a conversation with gods themselves. I wanted them to see the truth for themselves. They listened to my request, and 2 editors came to my house, and as a result they were able to see the content of this book in front of them and understand it. They said that they were glad they came, and that they did not expect the book to be so amazing. Their faith in God became stronger. There were 2 gods accompanying each of them also.

After our meeting, we asked Amaterasuoomikami-sama where he was before being there. The answer that came from Amaterasuoomikami-sama was "Re-e-ta-ki-ru-na-ke-i-a-a-ya-fu-ha-sa," composed of 14 Japanese letters.

There were 6 of us, 2 from Tama Publishing, the other 4 including myself and my members. We thought and thought about what that statement meant, but could not figure it out. But through some questions we were able to discern the purpose of the statement.

"Re-e-ta-ki-ru-na-ke-i-a-a-ya-fu-ha-sa is not about a location, but has something to do with the moon in the universe. Please include this word in the book you are publishing. There is meaning in it." This was the message I received, so I have written it down.

I still do not fully understand the meaning of this word, so if there is anybody who does, or has something that can be a hint, please teach me about it. I would like to confirm with Amaterasuoomikami-sama about the information. Thank you.

Chapter 7

Seventeen-years history of Future Waves

In this chapter I will talk about the history of the past 17 years of Future Waves, how it has progressed.

August 1st 2000, I encountered the wave measurement device and the magnetic necklace. As I made a decision on the purchase, an expert who can use the device came with me. The necklace was made out of a precious metal with magnetic platinum, approved by the government as a medical tool for its ability to improve blood flow.

I became able to detect problems with the wave measurement device, then improve the condition using the magnetic necklace, with results verified. Eventually I encountered a necklace that had 4 times the ability of the magnetic necklace I had initially. I confirmed it with the wave measurement device. When I saw the president of the company that sold this necklace, he said that the spiritual side must be observed, not just the necklace, or otherwise conditions will not improve. So then I began to take an interest in the unseen.

He taught me how to deal with spirits also. The method was to lay salt on my palm, grind it, then toss it outside after twisting it. However, this method could not be performed indoors, and children could not perform it, so I had them carry the salt wrapped in tissue paper. Then I would enhance the waves of the salt, and use other tools to remove anything harmful to the body, where then the harmful things would come out of the hand. Not only spirits, but bacteria, viruses, and harm done by drugs would also come out, which was good.

However, with this method, the spirits, bacteria, and viruses in the salt will not be purified. When I asked a psychic, I was told to throw away accumulated salt in the river after removing the tissue paper. I was not only worried what people would think when they saw me do this, but to throw away salt contaminated with spirits, bacteria, and viruses in to the river did not seem like a good thing to me. I even felt spirits following me from behind after putting the salt in the river, which was uncomfortable. Then another psychic told me that if I use a stone with high waves, the contamination will disappear. I experimented, and found that it was true, which made me extremely thankful.

So, as I received advice from many people, I stepped deeper and deeper in to the realm of the unseen. I will show my activities in a timeline.

● my activities in a timeline

2000	Encounter with the wave measurement device and the magnetic necklace. Discovery made regarding effects of magnetic necklace, and begin searching for methods beyond just putting it around the neck, for its application.
Aug 11 2005	First book "The Truth of Life Revealed by Waves" published (Tama Publishing).
April 1 2010	Second book "What Disease Really Are, Shown by Future Waves" published (Tama Publishing).

Jan 2011	A member from Yamaguchi prefecture sends a picture of a grassy field with a fox spirits and cat spirit. After cleaning the premises and giving offerings to the spirits, and going back from there for the 3rd time, a member takes a photograph of the clouds reaching high altitudes in the sky. After studying the photo, a fox and cat are detected, and the numbers match what they were after the purification. After many verifications, the relationship between clouds and the ascension of spirits is discovered.
2012	Medicine given at the hospital through injection over and over turned out to be harmful, and there is success to purify it through the neck. The magnetic necklace is put on the affected areas while having salt placed in the palm of 1 hand, and the harm of the medicine went in to salt immediately with the pain subsiding. The person exclaimed "It's magic!" With this as a hint, a new purification method using the magnetic necklace begins.
April 15 2012	In the morning the phone rings and it is from Nagoya, 30 kilometers away. "There is a white line rising in the sky towards Okazaki so please take a picture" was the message. After looking at it, I realized that it was from the spirits that were here from Yamaguchi the other day, and they were ascending to the heavens. It was emotional about seeing this occurrence so clearly for the first time.
Oct 28 2012	Hurricane Sandy lands on the U.S. Hundreds of thousands of people evacuate, and there is an enormous damage. I measured a picture of it and found 21 Satanic snake spirits with neurological disturbance, alcoholism, anger, and stress. The reason snakes are stressed and angry must be because they are put into alcoholic beverages alive and turned in to analeptics.

Nov 29 2012	On the day of the session of the School of Waves, right on top of the session hall there was an upside down rainbow. I measured the rainbow, and saw that the spirits, bacteria, and viruses of the people I purified that day had all ascended to the heavens, and were in the rainbow. Later I found out that Seoritsuhime-sama and Tahataraketen-god were at the opposing ends of the rainbow when it was made. Then we found out that those who ascended to the heavens were going in to the rainbow.
Feb 2013	The truth about the chem trail, a poly tank with bacteria and viruses was loaded on to an airplane that emits toxins from midair, is revealed. At the point of emission there is an outbreak of a norovirus, measles, and the flu. After measuring the poly tank and smoke in the airplane, the causes of the diseases are detected. Who are the people emitting these and profiting?
Aug 28 2013	On day where a session for the School of Waves was held, the face of Kanzeon Bosatsu-sama (Seoritsuhime-sama and Tahataraketenkami-sama) appear. (refer to Chapter 2 "Ro-Ne-Ra-Wa-Yu-Wa (Conversations with Gods) / Seoritsuhime-sama)
May 18 2014	While watching a debate on television, I implemented long-distance hand power on the politicians. I checked how it worked, and whatever that was possessing them disappeared. Afterwards, on a day where a session of the School of Waves was held, I selected the people who were at the top of the world and implemented hand power. As we continued, we found that some people's hands would begin hurting, or that they would be affected negatively from the other side, so we stopped.
Nov 16~18 2014	We went to try purifying the radiation at Minamisoma City in Fukushima prefecture. Ever since the disaster of March 11th 2011 in eastern Japan, mountains of polluted soil became an issue. Thinking that time and

	money could be saved by placing stones and soil on surfaces to purify them, we studied countless samples of stones to see which one would be suitable for purification, and selected a few types. We tested their effects together with people from an NGO. The radiation would be gone for the measurement, but would get stuck with the Geiger counter, or the sound will go off because of reacting to what's in the air. The results were not convincing for people.
Dec 1 2014	I received 3 stamps of approval at the notary office. Regarding the experiment to remove cesium and other activities at Minamisouma City… The content of the progress report included 2 sheets of the progress document, 3 sheets of the results of analysis, and the thesis which was 9 sheets of paper in A4 size. Regarding the methods involving the things possessing people, animals, plants, food, etc., where they are being a negative influence but become adsorbed by magnetism, or disassembled and put in to salt with high waves, and thereby improvement is made. The content is a thesis with 6 sheets of writing and 11 sheets of photos. A thesis with 42 photos, 11 sheets of writing, and pictures analyzed of 7 people where their blood was blown up to 3600 times. A needle was applied to the finger where a drop of blood came out.
Jan 26 2015	The Card of Hikari (the light of God) is completed after trial and error. During this time polluted water in a tank in Fukushima had become a serious problem. There was no place to put it and the polluted water would leak. Because of this it was obvious how much cesium, uranium, and plutonium were in the tank, where and how much, after taking a picture of the tank from outside. It was possible to purify them in 2 ~ 3 minutes.

July 23 2015	Three consecutive typhoons occur with typhoons 9, 10, and 11. I attain the understanding around this time that many spirits are expressing their crazed anger like an explosion in typhoons. This is especially true regarding the spirits of animals who have been used for food. Afterwards I began purifying spirits, bacteria, and viruses and having them ascend to the heavens.
Aug 6 2015	There was a broadcast of a special program because it had been 70 years after the war. It was about the hellish suicidal missions in Ioushima Island . The spirits of the young people who gave their lives to their country remained there along with their pain, burns, and feelings. I purified the picture of Ioushima Island , and many were released from their pain and suffering, rising high in to the sky of Okazaki.
Oct 19 2015	Purification of the Tottori earthquake is done. The earthquakes which had been occurring over and over cease immediately. (refer to Chapter 6 The Way of Salvation is to Surrender to the Guidance of God / the cause of the Tottori earthquake)
Nov 29 2015	I put my beloved cat Musashi, who had been in pain, to sleep.
2015	end of the year I put all my thoughts regarding radiation, evil spirits, bacteria, viruses, and the practice and application of the Card of Hikari and its accomplishments in to a thesis.
Feb 11 2016	Stamps of approval are given at the notary office for the thesis regarding the influenza virus, the discovery of its causes, and a solution to the problem. There were 11 sheets of writing and 7 photos in the thesis.
April 14 2016	An earthquake occurs in Kumamoto at 9:26pm. Although purification is performed abundantly, the earthquakes occur ceaselessly. Confirmation is made through the gods that there is a relationship between

	animal spirits and the earthquakes. (refer to Chapter 6 The Way of Salvation is to Surrender to the Guidance of God / cause of Kumamoto earthquakes)
April 17 2016	The 2nd experiment in Fukushima is performed to see if the Card of Hikari can remove radiation. Same as before, the removal could be made, but due to a problem with the Geiger counter, an accurate measurement could not be made.
April 20 2016	The power of the Card of Hikari increased, so spirits, bacteria, and viruses could be identified just with a photograph of the face. Then the style changed to purifying only with a photo of the forehead, and the process becomes simplified.
April 25 2016	I begin to take walks with the 4 ancestors of the Nomura family every day. (refer to Chapter 4 The Afterlife / Daily life of ancestors and conversations with them)
May 7 2016	Conversations with ancestors begin. (same as previous date)
May 18 2016	First conversation with the Kanzeon Bosatsu-sama whose face appeared in the sky.
May 23 2016	Conversation with the 4 spirits that were upstairs. (refer to Chapter 4 The Afterlife / Someone who lived in the second floor of our house)
May 24 2016	Conversations with angels. (refer to Chapter 3 A Dream Story and the Unknown World / conversations with angels)
June 16 2016	Conversation with someone who was a detective when he was alive. (refer to Chapter 4 the Afterlife / What was bothering the person who was a detective when he was alive?)
July 11 2016	Conversations with cosmic beings (2 women from Planet Reyaeronarahoo)

Aug 29 2016	I find out that the name of Kanzeon Bosatsu-sama comes from Seoritsuhime-sama and Tahataraketen-sama)
Aug 30~31 2016	The truth regarding the 16 princes, Japan being the prototype of the world, Amanoiwatobiraki, and Amaterasuoomikamisama, are revealed. (refer to Chapter 2 Ro-Ne-Ra-Wa-Yu-Wa (Conversations with Gods) / the light coming from the east is about this light of God)
Aug 2016	I start being able to notice gods accompanying people by studying the waves of the person's forehead.
Sep 2016	Conversations with gods accompanying me and my grandson.
Oct 6 2016	On this day I discovered that the information in my forehead is divided in to 14 layers. (later I find more layers)
Nov 3 2016	The Kanzeon Bosatsu-sama creates a new Card of Hikari after I ask.
Nov 25 2016	I observe the new wave measurement device. A person who had been hospitalized many times because of heart disease said "It's no good just being told that there's something wrong with my heart. I already know that. What I need is for my heart to get better!" and went home. I felt that Future Waves truly was better than modern devices.
Jan 1 2017	A visitor from Tottori. (refer to Chapter 1 Cause of Illness Can Be Found Deep Within the Third Eye / the truth which was discovered through the mortuary tablet)
Jan 23 2017	The death of my cat Sasuke (refer to Chapter 4 The Afterlife / thanks to my 100 year old beloved cat)

Feb 9 2017	God asks me to help someone. (refer to Chapter 3 A Dream Story and the Unknown World / How a god entered in to my dream which then came true.)
Feb 10 2017	From studying the people around me and celebrities, I find out that some people have foreheads with 20 layers or even 50 layers.
March 10 2017	I became unable to use my wrist from its fracture, pain, and swelling.
April 1 2017	I learned in detail about cosmic beings (37 gods) from having a conversation with gods.
April 6 2017	From televised images I find a spirit group consisting of 33 spirits near a ship around North Korea. While being supervised by gods (60 gods), I brought them to my house and had a conversation. (refer to Chapter 2 Ro-Ne-Ra-Wa-Yu-Wa (Conversations with Gods) / purification of spirit groups)
April 8 2017	Discovery made of 402 spirits in a spirit group at the United Nations Security Council, then purified. There were 1500 gods at my house during this time. (same as previous date)
April 12 2017	The message that the human world must be figured out by humans alone, and that gods can't interfere is given by 2023 gods. (refer to Chapter 2 Ro-Ne-Ra-Wa-Yu-Wa (Conversations with Gods) / purification of plutonium)
April 13 2017	Using satellite images, radiation and vast amounts of plutonium are found in North Korea. Then 3500 gods said that purification will undo the hazard, and it is done. (same as previous date)
April 16 2017	I become quite busy with purifying important people of the world every day. There were 20488 gods this day. They answered that they were there to participate

	in a joyful event. (refer to Chapter 2 Ro-Ne-Ra-Wa-Yu-Wa (Conversations with Gods) / more than 37000 gods!)
April 20 2017	The number of gods became 37622.
April 23 2017	Two spirit groups found with satellite images, and conversations with them are held at my house. 32240 gods.
April 26 2017	The title of this book "A New World With God!" is decided by 28955 gods.
April 28 2017	As the end of the month became near, many gods went back to their own areas and the number became 19992 gods.
April 30 2017	We are told by 8045 gods what to do from hereon.
May 3 2017	I was marveled because I was told that Jesus, Buddha, and Mohammed were present in my house. (refer to Chapter 2 Ro-Ne-Ra-Wa-Yu-Wa (Conversations with Gods) / Christ, Mohammed, and Buddha)
May 4 2017	Jesus answers questions asked by members of the School of Waves who studied Christianity.
May 6 2017	Four hundred gods say that they would like to have me read them my notes, so I do so after asking them where I should start reading from.
May 14 2017	Iron balls come falling, and a message is sent by God. (refer to Chapter 2 Ro-Ne-Ra-Wa-Yu-Wa (Conversations with Gods) Iron balls come falling
May 17 2017	Conversation with Kotama Okada, the founder of the Mahikari organization. (same as previous date)
My 19 2017	The discovery is made that the Cosmic God is at the pinnacle and that God is an organization of gods like a pyramid. I asked the names of the remaining gods in the world. (refer to Chapter 2 Ro-Ne-Ra-Wa-Yu-Wa (Conversations with Gods) the story of the 16 princes)

May 20 2017	In Sri Lanka, 101 Satanic spirits are purified.
May 23 2017	Three who are all Daikoku-sama appear for a visit in the front entrance of my house. (refer to Chapter 2 Ro-Ne-Ra-Wa-Yu-Wa (Conversations with Gods) / cosmic spirits and their increase)
May 26 2017	A surprising visit from Susano-o-sama, the Jinmu Emperor, Master Shinran, and Master Rennyo. (Chapter 2 Ro-Ne-Ra-Wa-Yu-Wa (Conversations with Gods) / the legend of Yamato no Orochi, Susano-o-sama)
May 28 2017	I learn the names of gods. Kukai, Saicho, Master Ippen shounin, 2 Ebisu gods, 11 gods from Plate engraving Lotus Sutra Mandala and 15 gods from Kongokaimandara , along with some living gods including the 17th, 18th, and 19th emperors, 3 descendants, and another. (same as previous)
June 6 2017	I find out that the supreme god Amaterasuoomikami-sama is in my miniature shrine in my house. (Chapter 2 Ro-Ne-Ra-Wa-Yu-Wa (Conversations with Gods) / Amaterasuoomikami-sama)
June 7 2017	More names of gods are revealed. From a genealogy of gods, 17 gods and 20 living gods including the Ankan Emperor and their names are told. (Chapter 2 Ro-Ne-Ra-Wa-Yu-Wa (Conversations with Gods) / 37 gods)
June 14 2017	Okuninushi-sama tells me the truth of the legend of the white Inaba rabbit. (refer to Chapter 2 Ro-Ne-Ra-Wa-Yu-Wa (Conversations with Gods) / Okuninushi-sama)
June 14 2017	The gods tell me who will make the shrine necessary for the 200 gods to be in. (refer to Chapter 2 Ro-Ne-Ra-Wa-Yu-Wa (Conversations with Gods) / to be completely guided by God)

July 6 2017	The 376 Plus Satanic spirits who were at the United Nations Security Council are called from Mercury and they talk about the progress Mercury is making.
July 7~14 2017	The Anacondas are asked to calm the heavy rain in Kyushu. (refer to Chapter 3 A Dream Story and the Unknown World / the bond between the cosmic spirit and the anaconda)
July 14 2017	The anaconda family was reunited.
July 27 2017	The health product I wanted to drink was gone. A true kamikakushi.
Aug 1 2017	A revelation from God was given (komiwarete…)
Aug 1 2017	Typhoon 5 occurred, and the anacondas who helped with the Kyushu heavy rain once again helped.
Aug 5 2017	I asked 4 dragon gods to help with Typhoon 5 because it was a strong typhoon.
Aug 9 2017	I called the 4 dragon gods, 2 dragons, 5 anacondas, and 3 big snakes over to thank them regarding Typhoon 5.
Sep 16 2017	It was reported that Typhoon 18, an enormous size, will land on Kyushu. Along with the dragon gods who helped with Typhoon 5, I asked 1 male dragon god and 6 female dragon gods from western Australia to help also.
Sep 19 2017	I brought all the ones who helped with Typhoon 18 (11 dragon gods, 2 dragons, 5 anacondas, 7 big snakes) to thank them.
Sep 28 2017	Discovery of a genetically engineered cell is made, and a conversation with it from its heart is heard for the first time.
Oct 2 2017	Confirmation is made about whether the cells exist inside the food in my house.
Oct 8 2017	I write several letters to politicians about this fact.

Oct 10 2017	When asking cosmic spirits about where they have come from, I was able to have a conversation with those from Planet Yuromuromu. This was the seventh planet where I learned its name.
Oct 16 2017	I called 38 spirits from North Korea, and asked how things had been going. I attained the information that 4 new missiles had been made, and though it was not complete, many of its parts were being arranged, and they were getting nuclear material that was initially planned to be discarded.
Oct 21 2017	The enormous Typhoon 21 was coming, and I asked those who helped with Typhoon 18 to also help with this typhoon so that it will not damage Japan.
Oct 23 2017	The enormous Typhoon 23 changed its course ad headed towards the Pacific Ocean, which was against the forecast. This made me realize the greatness of the dragon gods. I thanked them with the others who were heling with the publication.
Oct 27 2017	I had a conversation with something that was possessing my member after I purified them, and the 2 of them said that their pain would not ease no matter what, so I listened closely. (refer to Chapter 4 The Afterlife / Conversation with a satanic spirit who dwelled inside blood)
Oct 27 2017	There was news that Typhoon 22 changed its course. I thought that perhaps the dragon gods had made that happen, and it turned out that I was right as I confirmed their presence in Japan through satellite images.
Oct 28 2017	I called the Phoenix over and asked some questions (refer to Chapter 3 The Dream Story and the Unknown World / The anaconda which became reunited with its family.)

Oct 29 2017	I inquired the gods about the cover of the book and the band to go around it. They said to change the title of Chapter 2 from "Conversations with Gods" to "Ro-Ne-Ra-Wa-Yu-Wa (Conversations with Gods)." Ro-Ne-Ra-Wa-Yu-Wa means "conversations with gods" in katakamuna, according to the gods. I was taught this by 478 gods.
Nov 8 2017	I called the 38 spirits from North Korea and asked what has been happening. Two out of the 4 missiles have become complete. The used nuclear material still is not in possession. They have ambitions to use the nuclear missile in the ocean for the purpose of threat. Inconveniences in the lives of citizens are arising.

"I have received a final message from the Space Creator deity"

Final Message from the Space Creator deity (King of the Gods, Amaterasuoomikami, Seikannon, YHVH, Jehova and Allah)

In religions, the Space Creator deity is referred to as Master God, Amaterasuoomikami, Seikannon, YHVH, Jehova, or Allah, according to nation and region. The root of religions is one, and God is the same. This means that if there is war between different branches of religion, it would go against the will of God.

Currently, the founders of all religions are all here in my house, and are hoping that people will all come to this realization. If you'd like, you can speak to any of the founders, so please let me know.

Recently, the Space Creator deity has informed me of the disturbance in the geological axis and about natural disasters. It was quite important, so I asked about it further.

On March 2nd, 3rd, and 4th of 2018 I listened to the Creator until I understood fully. This message is the last one from the Creator, having to do with the survival of the universe and the planet. The natural disasters that are about to occur will become our worst case scenario, different from all the ones we have faced before. The Space Creator deity would like to reveal the facts to everybody. I will give them one by one.

First I asked about the origin of the universe

① The many stars inside our vast universe were made out of energy which caused the Big Bang.

② The Space Creator deity accomplished this alone.

③ Out of the many stars, the sun was created so that it would emit heat.

④ Gold, silver, aluminum, iron, and copper were put inside the stars as resources when they were created.

⑤ The ocean was created, and the parents of tens of thousands of fish were created with it.

⑥ The mountain was created, and tens of thousands of vegetation and flowers were created.

⑦ Tens of thousands of animals were created.

⑧ After creating everything, the Creator divided its soul in to 7 components, and created humans (god-children).

⑨ Humans (god-children) have been marrying and multiplying till this day. Humans are god-children.

The Space Creator deity said it divided its soul in to 7 components. I asked the names of the 7 gods (in relation to the human world)

Eldest Son Mehachitenuhoseateshiutoanomikoto
Second Son Kamimusubinokami
Third Son Fumifusoowahitsuwanekami
Fourth Son Kiehiseamorichitatsuruhonomikoto
Fifth Son Okuninushinomikoto (Inaba no Shirousagi)
Sixth Son Kunitokotati-nomikoto (Hitsukishinji)
Seventh Son Susanoonomikoto (Yamatanoorochi)

① The second son, third son, fifth son, and seventh son are staying in my house.

② Okuninushinomikoto, the fifth son, is famous in the mythological tale of the Inaba no Shirousagi, but it turns out that half of it is made up.

③ Kunitokotati-nomikoto, the sixth son, is the god that made Okamoto Tenmei write what he wrote.

④ The seventh son, Susanoonomikoto, is famous for the story mythological tale of "Yamatanoorochi", but it turned out that half of it was made up. Also, the absolute god Narayana of the Mu Empire, who had 7 heads, was the same snake as Yamatanoorochi in Japanese mythology. After the sinking of the Mu Continent, it came to Japan, and I heard about the story of how

The cause of the sinking of the continents of Atlantis, Mu, and Lemuria

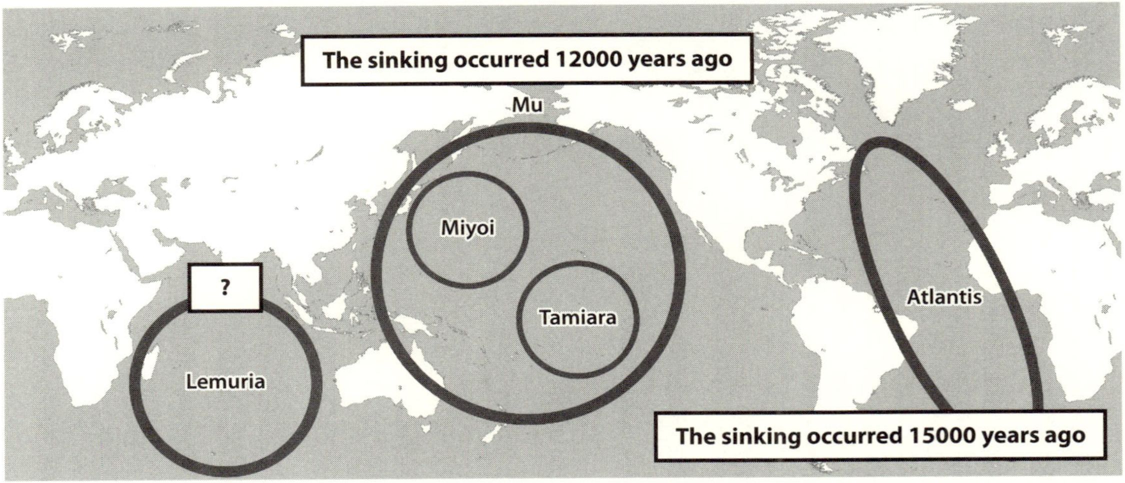

The Atlantis continent sank 15000 years ago, the Mu Continent sank 12000 years ago, and this is a fact. I was told that the cause of it is psychic negativity that leads to natural disasters. It is similar to our situation now! (If we keep going we will have natural disasters occurring.) The Lemuria continent also sank, but the cause of all of this is the imbalance in the geological axis. I was also told that the imbalance in the geological axis is caused by the typhoons, hurricanes, earthquakes, tsunamis, nuclear explosions, nuclear experimentation, and bombings during war that are caused by psychic negativity.

7 God divided the Spirit!

family relationship	name of a god	people whom God was possessed by
Eldest Son	Mehachitenuhoseateshiutoa nomikoto	Buddha, Mohammed, Jeanne d'Arc, Nakayama Miki (Tennrikyo), Nikola Tesla, Noguchi Hideyo Itokawa Hideo (aeronautical engineering)
Second Son	Kamimusubinokami	Abraham, Moses, Nichiren Shonin, Kamibito (Ôhitsukushinji)
Third Son	Fumifusoowahitsuwanekami	Deguchi Nao (Ômotokyo), Albert Einstein, Pablo Picasso, Okada Kôtama (Sekaimahikari-bunmeikyodan), Mother Teresa, Masaki Kazumi
Fourth son	Kiehiseamorichitatsuruho nomikoto	Deputy leader of the Space Creator deity (Right hand)
Fifth Son	Okuninushinomikoto (Inaba no Shirousagi)	Kûkai, Rennyo Shonin, Deguchi Onisaburou (Ômotokyo), Leonardo da Vinci
Sixth Son	Kunitokotatinomikoto	Thomas Edison, Okamoto Tenmei, Yukawa Hideki
Seventh Son	Susanoonomikoto (Yamatanoorochi)	Confucius, Jesus Christ, Shinran Shonin, Kosaka Wado (Takeuchi monjyo)

After the Sinking of the Mu Continent ~ History of Japan ~

The absolute god Naranaya of the Mu Empire, who has 7 heads

Yamatanoorochi / Slayed by Susanonomikotosama

Back when people of the Mu Continent were busy with war, there was the absolute god Naranaya who had 7 heads (snake), who came to Japan after the continent sank. In the mythological story about Yamatanoorochi, it is said that Susanonomikoto actually slayed Yamatanoorochi, which is famous. I had heard about this before, but I asked the gods if they are the same snake.

I received the answer "Yes" from Susanonomikotosama directly.
The gods, who are our ancestors, have been protecting us since ancient time. What can we give to the gods in return?

Susanoonomikoto slayed it.

⑤ The eldest, fourth son, and sixth son are gods that are managing the stars of the universe. The gods that came to be from the division of the soul of the Space Creator deity all do their job that they are qualified to do.

*Regarding the Hitsukishinji book

* The Hitsukishinji was written by Okamoto Tenmei, him working as a channelist through the god Kunitokotati-nomikoto. The book contains knowledge about Japan's defeat, the fire bombings of Tokyo, the collapse of the bubbling economy, the East Japan Disaster, and other things about the future which have all come true, and is said to be the best book of prophecies in Japan.
* The book talks about how the map of Japan is like a model of the world map. Africa is Kyushu, Australia is Shikoku, Eurasia is Honshu, and North America is Hokkaido. Even the shapes are similar. Also, Mt. Fuji is at the same location as the Himalayas, and Lake Biwa is at the same location as the Caspian Sea. The Japanese archipelago is a microcosm of the world, the origin of the human race, the spiritual prototype, the nation that is the origin of spirituality. All of the world would surely respond with agreeance. Along with this, there have

been discoveries of the chrysanthemum which is the symbol of the Japanese imperial family in various ancient sites around the world. From Japan, 16 princes were sent out to create nations, and the chrysanthemum symbol has 16 petals. This truth is beyond amazing, and there is no falseness in it.

The Japanese Islands are reduced drawings of the world

The birthplace of humanity
A country of spirit form / The original country of the spirit / Japan

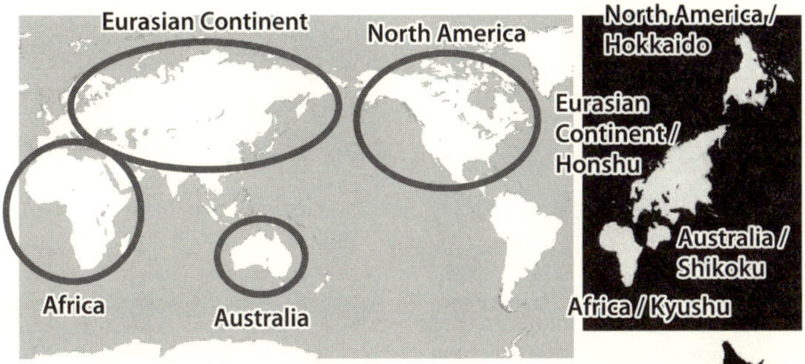

The 16 princes and the chrysanthemum emblem

Ancient city of the Mesopotamia region
"Ishtar Gate"

Egyptian Archeology Museum
"Chrysanthemum emblems found in the tomb of Tutankhamun."

Historical monument in Thatta, Pakistan "Ancient Sumerian"

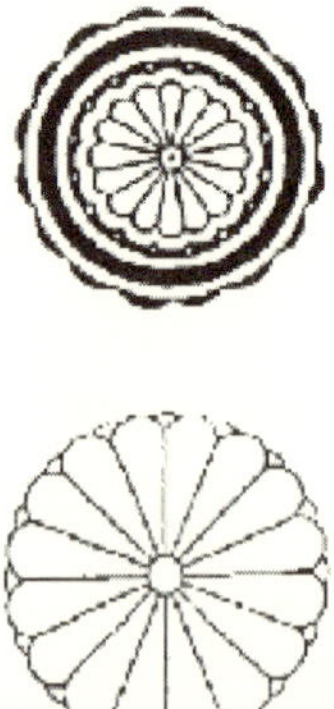

Emblem which is left in the North America Zuni tribe
Native American emblem

Sarcophagus of the Jewish King Herod
(He ruled it from B. C. 47 to A. D. 4.)

Is the content of the Hitsukishinji book true?

① It is true that Kunitokotati-nomikoto worked through Okamoto Tenmei to have it written.

② Kunitokotati-nomikoto wrote it, representing the Space Creator deity.

③ Kunitokotati-nomikoto is the sixth god of the 7 divisions of the soul of the Space Creator deity.

④ The content of the Hitsukishinji is mostly correct.

Regarding the tragic contents of the Hitsukishinji

① From the North, ○○○ and ○○will come to invade. (I will conceal who the invader is here.)

② After the invasion, Mt Fuji will erupt. The invaders will retreat.

③ When Jupiter becomes visible in the eastern skies, and about ten thousand people start dying daily, the end of the world will be near.

④ When the sun splits in to 4 parts, the world will end.

* I asked about the ten thousand people dying per day in number 3(③), and received the answer that the deaths would be causes by disasters and spirits, bacteria, viruses, and additives in the body, along with damages from drugs and poor cellular health.

* I asked about the sun splitting in to 4 parts in number 4(④), and received the answer that heat and light from the sun will be reduced to less than half as a result.
* There was also the answer regarding number 4(④) that the "end of the world" part is actually incorrect. I asked about it further, and learned that other planets besides Earth will be affected, that some parts of Japan will sink, that only 10% of people will survive, and that the survivors will have to do everything from scratch in a miserable environment.

In the prophecy, it is said that the Space Creator deity will come down to Earth, the material world, namely Japan. Would this be in order to prevent the disasters just discussed?

① Yes.
② For this reason, we have been waiting for the chance to use the wave device for thousands of years for there to be correspondence with gods.
③ If many people could choose to be better and put their minds towards God, we can also escape the natural disasters (The eruption of Mt. Fuji, the sun splitting in to 4 parts, etc.).

④ The eldest, fourth son, and sixth son are gods that are managing the stars of the universe. They make an effort in the restoration of the degree of leaning of the earth's axis, but a bad condition keeps not catching up with it. In this situation when we attacked it from the North, we become already out of control !

⑤ Currently, North Korea and the United States are not getting along, and there is danger of war breaking out.

⑥ The other day, from satellite images from around the world, I have found mercury and plutonium in more than 10 different locations.
It was said that I changed by just that much if I purified a nucleus, radioactivity.

⑦ If all the things that were found were purified now, explosions could be avoided in time of war.

⑧ After hearing about these things, I purified (removed them from the locations they were found) everything at 5:14pm on March 3rd 2018.

The next day on March 4th, I asked what was influencing the geological axis the most, since it worried me when I heard about it the day before

① Nuclear explosions

② Nuclear experimentation

③ Bombings during war

④ Missile launches

⑤ Nuclear power plants

⑥ Earthquakes (the ones caused by people)

⑦ Earthquakes (causes by the anger and stress of animals)

* Nuclear power plants operating normally still do affect the geological axis. They must be stopped, because disasters are going to happen more.
* There have been earthquakes more than tentimes caused by people using an explosive device. The ones causing this trouble are not foreigners but in fact Japanese, who are paying people who come with visas to do it for them.
* The nation of ○○ is causing disasters in Japan other than earthquakes. (It is not announced at present.)

Over a time span of 3 days, I learned much from the Space Creator deity, especially about upcoming natural disasters. The Space Creator deity and the earth, upon dividing its soul in to 7 components, has become unable to create anything at all. What this means is that there will be no god available to take care of the planet after it is ruined by natural disasters. Earth and humans will all just go down to hell. Beneath rubble, in the ocean, and in the sand for perhaps hundreds and thousands of years...though you will yell and scream, nobody will listen, and you will only suffer in pain, filled with regret. Even if you'd like to die, you can do nothing about it since you are already a soul. While alive, you can move around with your arms and legs, but if you become a spirit bound to your environment, there is no chance.

I have spoken with millions of souls, so I understand about the afterlife. I have removed human spirits, cosmic spirits, animal spirits, bacteria, viruses, and cells from their hell, cured their disease, and had them go home. They have experienced hell, so they listen to me intently, and have thankfulness.

Compared to this, many people in the actual world seem against things. However, God wants to communicate about the truth to people. People who get the information are free to interpret it as true or false. Please know that human greed to pursue material possessions has caused the endangerment of humanity and the planet.

If you start to change your way of thinking now and go ahead and become God's messenger, the universe and Earth can keep existing in their beauty the way they always have been.

From here on, I think the only way to move forward is to be guided by the Space Creator deity, the 7 divisions from its soul, the founders of the religions, and gods who have been born in to this world and have lead lives. There is much to keep in mind, but let's all do what we can individually do, change our behavior to be better, and move towards a new world with God to sustain our beautiful planet and universe!

In Closing

There are 500 gods in my house who answers questions for me every day. I myself have been accompanied by 2 gods, but this number increased and became 100.

With all of these gods present, it makes me worry that I cannot meet all of their expectations. But with the greatest leader in the world, with the greatest answer, believing that I have been given the greatest grace inside all of the universe, I have no fear or doubt.

Every day conversations with gods, spirits, cosmic spirits, animal spirits, bacteria, viruses, and Cells have been progressing, and when Typhoon 5 and 18 came along, I was able to seek help from dragon gods and dragons through conversation.

It has been 17 years since encountering and working with the unseen world, and I am convinced that progress with purification through waves will continue to be made. This can only be done with the light of God. The issues of the world now such as nuclear weapons, pollution, global warming, intractable disease, and disasters will all continue on to a point where they cannot be undone unless we do something about it.

Cosmic spirits and Cells inside of the food we eat are a cause of that and are a problem. When people eat the food the cosmic spirits and Cells become trapped inside of their blood, which results in them being in a state of hell. On the other hand, the people and animals who have them inside their blood will be affected by any sickness that the cosmic spirit or Cell has. Not only will medication not solve the problem, it will make it worse. If we leave this problem the way it is, in a few decades people will be in serious situations.

God in the heavens is observing this from above with a lot of worry, and has been sending many saints to the earth. However, human greed has not been decreasing, but getting worse. It is because there is still time to make things better that I, a person who loves Earth, has been chosen to have conversations with gods. From here on, with the guidance of God, I plan to spread the knowledge that people must purify themselves, and spread the practice of it.

Through the conversation with cosmic spirits, I was able to learn about the progress of Mercury. I wrote it in this book, but I was amazed that they have no wars there like they do here on Earth. I will ask spirits from Mercury why there are no wars there, what they have been doing to prevent it, and what we people from Earth can learn from them.

Diseases in this world that were unsolvable have been revealed of their nature from conversations with the unseen. Mysteries will become unraveled more and more. I hope that people who felt that the facts in this book are true will step forward together with God towards a better world, learn, take action, spread the truth. Let us create a world with no disease, pollution, or war. I hope it will happen as soon as possible. Let us relieve the gods of their worries they have been having for tens of thousands of years. It is up to each of us.

Please visit the website (kamitotomoni.jp) if you agree with the content of this book.

On the day of May 13, 2018, it has been revealed that great people in history who were not listed in this book are staying at my house.

☆Space Creator deity
☆It divided the Space Creator deity Spirit 7 God
☆Niniginomikoto
☆Emperor Jinmu
☆Emperor Meiji
☆Emperor Showa
☆Seoritsuhime
☆Moses
☆Jesus Christ
☆Buddha
☆Abraham
☆Pythagoras
☆Socrates
☆Michelangelo
☆Toyotomi Hideyoshi
☆Tokugawa Ieyasu
☆Isaac Newton
☆George Washington (The United States First President)
☆James Watt
☆Abraham Lincoln (The United States 16th President)
☆Sugihara Tiune (He was instructed by Okuninushi-

nomikoto)
☆Nelson Mandela
☆Sato Eisaku
☆Tezuka Osamu
☆Martin Luther King, Jr

Those great people who developed the world have come together to the Space Creator deity and watching where we are heading.

These lists are only a part. Many other great people have the same feeling.

They are longing for the day when their history built up by them becomes the theocracy aimed by God.

From the 6th volume, 9th chapter (pg 182) of Hitsukishinji

All is interdependence.
It must be understood that gods do not work alone and people do not work alone.

Explanation:
Unless God and people do not become united, the work of God cannot bare fruit.

God knows everything.
The truth is becoming revealed, both about the future and the past.
Let us entrust everything in God, the path that humanity must follow.

補足

※本書の日本語版である拙著「新しい世界　神とともに！」（たま出版）には掲載されていない追加部分の日本文を特別に掲載致します。

「宇宙創造神様より最後のメッセージを戴きました」

宇宙創造神（主の神、天照大神、聖観音、ヤハウェ神、エホバ神、アラー神）より最後のメッセージ

宗教では、宇宙創造神の御名を主の神、天照大神、聖観音、ヤハウェ神、エホバ神、アラー神などと、国や地域で呼び名の違いがありますが、宗教創設者の方々は、宇宙創造神のことをそれぞれのお名前で呼ばれています。宗教は元一つ、同じ神を崇拝されているのですから、宗門宗派などなく、ましてや宗教戦争などしたら、神様の御心に叛(そむ)いていることになるのです。

現在、わが家には全ての宗教の創設者の方々が勢揃いされていて、この事実をみなさまに気付いていただくことを待ち望んでおられます。ご希望の方は、どのような宗門宗派の創設者の方とでもお話しできますので、お申し出ください。

最近になって、宇宙創造神より、地軸のゆがみのことや天変地異のことをお聞きするようになり、大変重大なことでもあり、もっと詳しく順を追ってお聞きすることにしました。

2018年３月２日、３日、４日と３日間にわたり、納得ができるまでお聞きすることができました。この事実は、全世界の皆さんに聞いていただきたい、宇宙、地球の存続にも関わる宇宙

創造神からの最後のメッセージです。これから起こる天変地異は、今までと違って最悪の事態になるそうです。宇宙創造神も皆さんに事実をお伝えするようにおっしゃられました。お聞きしたことを、順に追ってお話しさせていただきます。

はじめに宇宙の成り立ちをお聞きしました

①途方もなく広大な宇宙の星の数々は、エネルギー（波動）がビッグバンを起こして出来上がったということです。

②宇宙創造神がそのことをお一人で実行されました。

③それぞれの星の中で、太陽は熱を発生させる役目として創造しました。

④それぞれの星の中に、金、銀、アルミ、鉄、銅……資源としての星々を創造されました。

⑤海を創造し、何万という魚の親を創造されました。

⑥山を創造し、何万という草木や花を創造されました。

⑦何万という動物も創造されました。

⑧全てのものを創造された後、ご自分の分け御霊を７つ創造され、人間（神の子）を創られました。

⑨人間（神の子）が結婚してどんどん増えて今日に至っています。

人類は皆神の子ということになります。

宇宙創造神は７つの分け御霊を創造されたとおっしゃられたので、創造された七神のお名前をお聞きしました（人間界の続柄では）

長男　めはちてぬほせあてしうとあ尊

次男　神皇産霊神（かみむすびのかみ）

３男　ふみふそおわひつわね神

４男　きゑひせあもりちたつるほ尊

５男　大国主尊（因幡の白兎）

６男　国常立尊（日月神示）

７男　素佐嗚尊（八岐大蛇）

①次男、３男、５男、７男の神は、わが家に滞在しておられます。

②５男の大国主尊は因幡の白兎の神話で有名ですが、半分は作り話とのことでした。

③６男の国常立尊は、岡本天明に自動書記を書かせた神です。

④７男の素佐嗚尊は八岐大蛇の神話で有名ですが、半分は作り話とのことでした。

また、７つの頭を持つムー帝国の絶対神ナラヤナが、日本の神話「八岐大蛇」と同じ蛇で、ムー大陸が沈んだ後日本に来たので、素佐嗚尊が退治されたことは直々にお聞きしました。

⑤長男、４男、６男の神は宇宙で星の運営をされておられるとのことです。

このように、宇宙創造神から直々に分け御霊を戴かれた神々は、それぞれの分野で大変ご活躍をしてくださっております。

アトランティス、ムー、レムリア大陸の沈没の原因

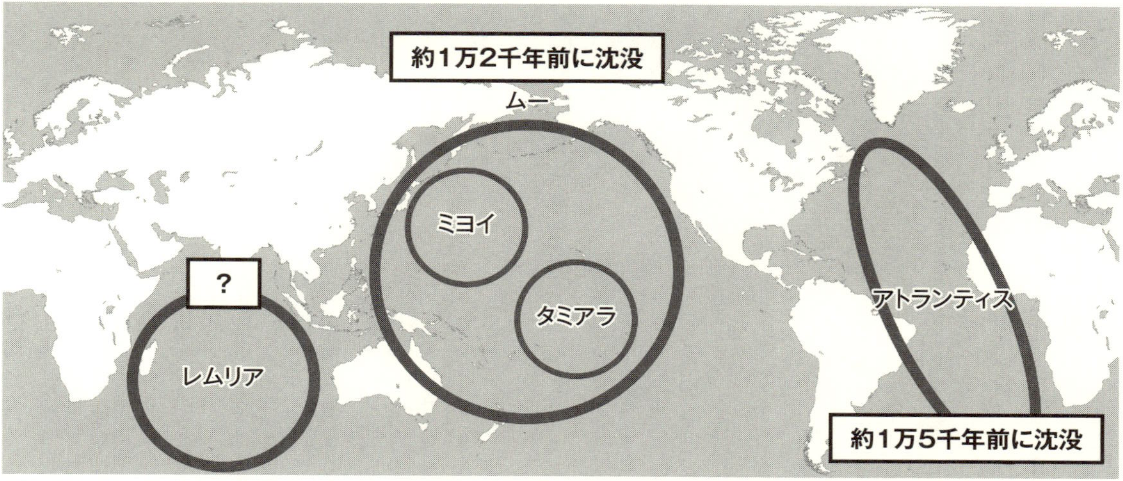

アトランティス約１万５千年前、ムー大陸が１万２千年前に沈没したのは事実とのお答えで沈没の原因とは、悪想念による天変地異で現在の状況と似ている！（このまま進むと天変地異が近づいている）他にレムリア大陸も同じく沈没したが、全て地軸のゆがみが原因です。また、地軸のゆがみは、人間の悪想念で起きる台風、ハリケーン、地震、津波。そして、核爆発、核実験、原子力発電、戦争による爆撃によってゆがみが起きてくる！とのお答えを戴きました。

世界を動かした宗教創設者や偉人には!

続柄	神様の御名前	神様がつかれた方々
長男	めはちてぬほせあてしうとあ尊	釈迦、マホメット、ジャンヌ・ダルク、中山みき(天理教)、ニコラ・テスラ、野口英世、糸川英夫(航空)
次男	神皇産霊神(かみむすびのかみ)	アブラハム、モーゼ、日蓮上人、神人(大日月地神示)
3男	ふみふそおわはつわね神	出口なお(大本教)、アインシュタイン、パブロ・ピカソ、岡田光玉(世界真光文明教団)、マザーテレサ、政木和三
4男	きゑひせあもりちたつるほ尊	宇宙創造神の副リーダー(片腕的存在)
5男	大国主尊(因幡の白兎)	空海、蓮如上人、出口王仁三郎(大本教)、レオナルド・ダ・ヴィンチ
6男	国常立尊(日月神示)	トーマス・エジソン、岡本天明、湯川秀樹
7男	素佐嗚尊(八岐大蛇)	孔子、イエス・キリスト、親鸞上人、高坂和導(竹内文書)

ムー大陸の沈没後〜日本の歴史〜

7つの頭を持つムー帝国の絶対神ナラヤナ

素佐嗚尊様が退治
—八岐大蛇—

ムー大陸が戦闘で明け暮れていた時、7つの頭を持つムー帝国の絶対神ナラヤナ(ヘビ)がいて、ムー大陸が沈んだ後、日本に来たそうです。日本の神話「八岐大蛇(やまたのおろち)」のお話で、実際、素佐嗚尊(すさのおのみこと)様が退治した有名な話があります。以前もそのお話が事実かどうかお聞きしたことがありますが、もしかしたら同一のヘビなのかお聞きしてみました。

素佐嗚尊様直々に「そうです」のお答えを頂きました。
このように、私たちの先祖にあたる神々が遠いいにしえから、子孫にあたる全人類を守り育んでくださっていたのです。
私たちはその神様方に感謝、お返しできることは何なのでしょうか?

※日月神示の本について

＊日月神示とは、岡本天明が国常立尊のお告げを自動書記によって書き、日本の敗戦や、東京大空襲、バブルが崩壊すること、東日本大震災などさまざまな未来を的中させ、日本の預言書では最もよく当たるといわれる書物のことです。

＊日本地図は世界地図のひな型になっていることもこの本に書かれています。アフリカが九州、オーストラリアが四国、ユーラシア大陸が本州、北アメリカが北海道とそのままそっくりです。その上、ヒマラヤ山脈と同じ位置に富士山が、カスピ海と同じ位置に琵琶湖があります。日本列島は世界の縮図、人類発祥の地、霊成型の国、霊の元つ国と言われています。世界の人々全員が見ても納得できる、今も存在している型です。その上、世界各地の古代遺跡から、日本の象徴である天皇家の菊型の御紋章が数多く発掘されています。日本から16人の皇子が世界に派遣されて国造りをされたとのことで、菊の御紋も16の花弁からなっています。これほどの真実はすごいことだと思います。全て嘘偽りのない証となっています。

日本列島は世界の縮図

人類発祥の地
霊成型の国　霊の元つ国　日本

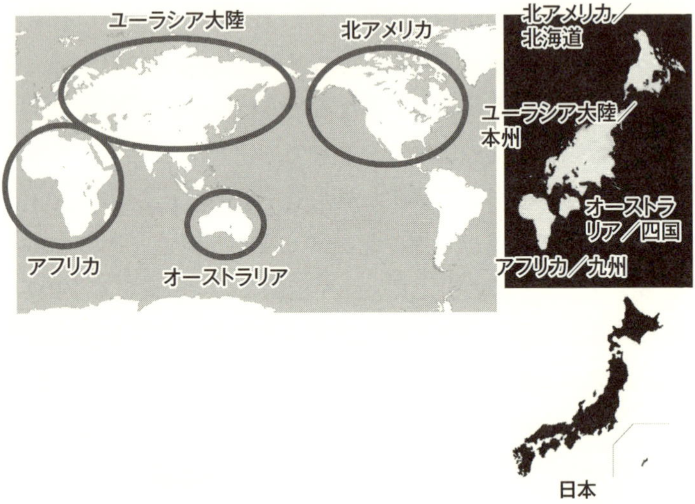

16人の皇子と菊型の御紋章

メソポタミア地方の古代都市「バビロンのイシュタル門」

エジプト考古学博物館「ツタンカーメンの墓から発見された菊の御紋」

パキスタンのタッタ遺跡「古代シュメール」

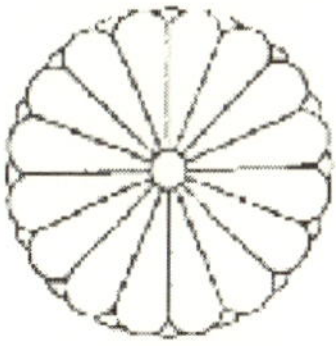

北アメリカ・ズニ族に残る御紋
ネイティブアメリカンの御紋

ユダヤのヘロデ王の石棺
（紀元前 47 年 ～ 紀元 4 年統治）

日月神示の本の内容は真実ですか?

①岡本天明が国常立尊のお告げで書いたのは事実です。

②国常立尊が宇宙創造神の代理で書いたものです。

③国常立尊は、宇宙創造神の７つの分け御霊の６番目の神です。

④日月神示の内容は、大体合っている。

日月神示に書かれている悲劇の内容です

①北の方から○○○、○○が攻めてきて占領される（ここでは伏せさせていただきます)。

②占領後、富士山が噴火し撤退する。

③金星が東の空に見えるようになったときに、１日10万人くらいずつ人が死に出したら世の終わりが近い。

④太陽が４つに分裂したら、この世の終わり。

＊③の、１日10万人くらいずつ人が死に出す、ということですが、どのような死に方ですか、とお聞きしたところ、災害と身体の中の霊、菌、ウイルス、添加物、薬害、細胞等の病気で死亡するとのお答えでした。

＊④の、太陽が４つに分裂したらどうなるのかをお聞きしたところ、太陽の熱と光が半分以下になるとのことです。

＊また、④の、“この世の終わり”の部分は違っている、とのお答えで、詳しくお聞きしたところ、地球以外の星にも影響する、地球の中で海の中に沈むところと、隆起するところがある、日本も沈むところがある、生き残る人は10％くらいである、生き残った人は、悲惨な環境の中、

一から出直すことになる、とのお答えでした。

予言では、宇宙創造神が物質界の地球に、特に日本にご降臨されると書かれていますが、このようなことを回避するために！ということなのでしょうか？

①はい、そうです。

②そのために、何千年前からこの波動器でしか解らない神との交信を待ち望んでいた。神には、この事実が見えていた。

③ここで、多くの皆さんが気付いてくれて、心を入れ替えて神とともに歩んでくれれば、すべての天変地異も免れることになります（富士山の噴火や太陽が４つに分裂すること等）。

④宇宙の方で星の運営を任されておられる長男、４男、６男の尊様方も、地軸の傾きの修復に努力はしておられるが、それに追いつかないほど悪条件が進んできている。このまま進んだら、北の方からの攻めが来きたとき、もう手の打ちようがなくなってくる！　という事態になってくる。

⑤現在、北朝鮮とアメリカが随分仲が悪くなってきていて、戦争にもなる危険もあります。

⑥先日、世界の衛星写真で、水銀、プルトニウムなどが10箇所以上見つかっています。核、放射能を浄化すれば、その分変わってくるとおっしゃられました。

⑦そして、現在見つけたものだけでも全部浄化しておけば、戦争になった場合爆発は避けることができるとのことでした。

⑧そのようなことをお聞きし、2018年３月３日午後５時14分より全て浄化（その場所から取り除く）致しました。

翌３月４日、昨日お聞きした地軸の傾きのことが心配でしたので、地軸の傾きに一番影響を与えているものとはどのようなことでしょうか？　とお聞きしました

①核の爆発
②核実験
③戦争の爆撃
④ミサイルの打ち上げ
⑤原子力発電
⑥地震（人間が起こしている）
⑦地震（主に動物の怒り、ストレスから起きた地震）

＊原子力発電は、正常な稼動でも地軸に影響がある。またこれから災害がどんどん起きてくるので、すぐ止めるべきです。

＊地震でも、人間が爆破装置を仕掛けて起きた地震が10回以上ある。犯人は外国人ではなく日本人がビザで来ている人にお金を払ってやってもらっている。単に自分の予知が当たることの証明のため。

＊地震以外に、日本に災いを起こしている国○○もある（ここでは伏せさせていただきます）。

３日間にわたり、主に宇宙創造神様より差し迫っている天変地異のことを詳しくお聞きしました。宇宙創造神様は、７つの分け御霊を創造されてから後、いっさい創造することができなくなっておられるそうです。ということは、例えば地球が天変地異を起こして分裂しても今度はそれを修正してくださる神はいません。地球も人間も全て地獄に行くだけです。ビルの下敷き、海の中、土砂の中で何百年か何千年か解りませんが、皆地獄で呼べど叫べど答えてもらえず、痛い、苦しい、後悔だけの何千年かが続くのです。死にたいと思っても既に死んでいて魂だけなのですから、何もできないのです。生きていれば手も足もあり、好きな所へもいけますが、地縛霊の魂はそこから動くこともできないのです。

私は、何百万もの魂と対話をしてきていますので、死後の様子はお聞きしております。人間霊も、宇宙霊も、動物霊も、菌も、ウイルスも、細胞も全て地獄から出してあげ、病気も改善させ、それぞれ故郷に帰るようにお話ししています。地獄の苦しさは一番よく体験されておられた方たちなので、こちらの言うことをよく解ってくれて、全員が素直に感謝できる方たちです。

それに比べ、現界の方々は、反対の方々が多いように思われます。ただ神様は、まだこの事実を聞きたいと待ち望んでいる方々がおられるので、お伝えしていくようにとおっしゃられています。お伝えを聞かれた方は、この事実を嘘と捉えても、真実と捉えてもよいのです。選ぶのは自由です。現在人間が物質を追い求めた、強欲の結果が人類破滅、地球破壊になってしまったことに気付いてください。

今からでも考えを改め、神様の伝言を実行していけば、宇宙も地球も美しいまま存在していくことができるとおっしゃってくださっています。

これからは、宇宙創造神、７つの分け御霊の神、全ての宗教創設者、人間として生まれ人生経験をされた神々など、数えきれない神々に教えていただきながら前に進んでいくことが、残された最後の道だと思っています。課題は多いですが、ご自分ができることに参加し、宇宙も地球もいつまでも美しく存続してもらうためにも、今まで間違ってきた過去の過ちを正し、新しい世界を神とともに築いていきましょう！

おわりに

わが家には日々、私の行動、質問にお答えしてくださる、500神以上の神様がおられます。また、私自身も２神から日々増加し、気がつくと100神もの神様に見守られていました。

こんなに多くの神様に来ていただき、それだけのご期待にお応えできるのだろうかという心配もあります。しかし、最強の指導者がおられて、最高の答えがあるのだから、壮大な宇宙の中で誰よりも恩恵を受けていると信じれば、迷いも恐れもなくなってきます。

日々、神様・霊・宇宙霊・動物霊・菌・ウイルス・細胞君との対話が進む中、台風５号、18号のときには、今まで写真でしか見たことのなかった竜や竜神様と対話して、お願いまで聞き入れていただけました。

見えない世界に取り組んで17年になりますが、これからも波動浄化の進歩は果てしなく続くでしょう。これも神様の光がなかったらできません。現在、世界を騒がせている核問題、汚染、温暖化、難病、災害など、このまま進んでしまったらもう手のつけられない状態になってしまいます。

その原因でもあり、身近な問題でもあるのが、食品中に紛れ込んだ細胞君、瞬間移動で地球上にやってくる宇宙霊です。食べた人の身体の中に入る彼らはその人が亡くなるまで血液の中で出口のない地獄の日々。いっぽうで身体の中に入って来られた方や動物は、入ってきた細胞君や宇宙霊が精神や病気を持っていれば、まったく同じ影響を受けます。難病であればあるほど、入られた人は苦しくなります。病院に行っても対症療法が多いので原因もわかりません。薬を飲んでも効かないどころか、さらに悪化するだけです。この状態を放置しておいたら、数十年後、ほとんどの人が大変な事態になっているでしょう。

神様も天上界からこの事実を見て、ご心配の種が絶えず、多くの聖者を世に送られてきました。しかし、人間の強欲は限りなく、悪化の一途をたどるばかり。今ならまだ間に合うからこそ、神様とお話ができるようになり、地球をとても愛している私が神様とのご縁をいただいたのだと思います。これからは「新しい世界　神とともに！」という本書のタイトル通り、神様直々のお力をお借りしながら、自分たちで浄化をする必要性を知ってもらい、実践を勧める活動を広めていくつもりです。

宇宙霊との対話から、地球より進化している水星の事情を知りました。本書で書きましたが、すごいなと思ったのは、地球のような戦争がないことです。どうして戦争が起こらないのか、そのためにどう工夫してきたのかを、これから水星の霊魂にお聞きして、地球人が見習うべきものをたくさん教えていただこうと思います。

世界中で解明できない病気の原因は、目に見えない世界との会話によって解き明かされてきました。これからもっと謎は明らかになるでしょう。本書の内容に真実を感じて、自分も神様とともに新しい世界を歩みたいと思われた方は、一緒に学び、実践し、この事実を世界に広げて、病気、汚染、戦争のない世界を目指していきましょう。

ゆくゆくは新しい実践の場が世界各地に出来て、それぞれが神様のお言葉を伝えてくだされば世界は変わるでしょう。それが１日も早く実現してほしいと思います。何万年も心配していただいている神様方に、安らかなお気持ちを持っていただける日を早く実現して差し上げたい。そんな私の願いは、皆さんお一人お一人のお気持ち次第で決まるのです。

この本を読まれご賛同くださった方は、ホームページ（https://kamitotomoni.jp/）をご覧ください。

※2018年５月13日現在　本の中に記載されていない歴史上の偉大な方々がこちら（野村家）におられる事実が確認できました。

☆宇宙創造神
☆宇宙創造神の分け御霊７神
☆迩迩芸命
☆神武天皇
☆明治天皇
☆昭和天皇
☆瀬織津姫
☆モーゼ
☆イエス
☆釈迦
☆アブラハム
☆ピタゴラス
☆ソクラテス
☆ミケランジェロ
☆豊臣秀吉
☆徳川家康
☆アイザック・ニュートン
☆ジョージ・ワシントン（アメリカ合衆国初代大統領）
☆ジェームズ・ワット
☆エイブラハム・リンカーン（アメリカ合衆国第16代大統領）
☆杉原千畝（大国主尊様がおつきになってご指導されました）
☆ネルソン・マンデラ

☆佐藤栄作
☆手塚治虫
☆キング牧師

世界中の皆様がよくお聞きになられたことのある歴史を塗り替えてこられた偉人の方々が、宇宙創造神のもとに集結され今後の行く末を見守ってくださっておられます。

また、ここに記載させていただいたのは一部で、まだまだたくさんの偉人の方々が同じお気持ちで、自分たちが築き上げてきた歴史が神様の目指す神政政治になれる日を待ち望んでおられます。

〜日月神示　第六巻　第９帖（一八二）より〜

「何事ももちつもたれつであるぞ。
神ばかりではならず人ばかりではならずと申してあろうが」

解説：神と人が一体（＝神人一体）にならなければ
神仕組みは何も成就しない。

〜・〜・〜・〜・〜・〜・〜・〜・〜・〜・〜・〜・〜・〜・〜・〜・〜

神は全てをご存知です。
未来も過去も次々と真実が明らかになってくる。
人類の進むべき道　全ては神にゆだねよう！

Author Biography

Fumiko Nomura

- Born December 18 1947
- Sagittarius／O blood type／from Fukui prefecture
- Had continual success with product ideas relating to being a house wife, 27 years ago.
- Encountered waves 17 years ago, and discovered the cause of misfortune and disease through her own ideas and research, and instructed how to remove the problem with simplicity. Mainly, spirits, bacteria, and viruses would be detected using Future Waves, and would be sent to Heaven with futuristic science.
- August 2005 "The Truth about Life Revealed with Waves" published (Tama Publishing)
- April 2010 "The True Nature of Disease taught by Future Waves" published (Tama Publishing)
- Currently is chairwoman of the fellowship "Miraihadojissen" (The Practice of Future Waves)

A New World with God!

2018年6月28日　初版第1刷発行

著　者　Fumiko Nomura
翻　訳　マルク・カーペンター
発行者　韮澤 潤一郎
発行所　株式会社 たま出版
〒160-0004 東京都新宿区四谷4－28－20
☎ 03-5369-3051（代表）
http://tamabook.com
振替　00130-5-94804

組　版　一企画
印刷所　株式会社エーヴィスシステムズ

ISBN978-4-8127-0417-2　C0011